My Healing Journey from Anxiety
A Divine Intervention

Shellie Goree Smith

Cover design by James Hammond, Art of Zen Designs

Table of Contents

To **my mom** *who taught me the power of Faith,*
Prayer, and God

To **my dad** *who showed me the importance of*
Strength and Perseverance

To **my husband** *who reminded me how to*
Love and Trust again

To **my sons** *who gave me back my Joy*

Introduction

According to the National Alliance of Mental Illness (NAMI) anxiety disorders are the most common mental health concerns in the United States. Over forty million adults (19.1%) have an anxiety disorder, however close to 75% of them either don't know they have it or refuse to seek treatment. All anxiety disorders have one thing in common: persistent, excessive fear or worry in situations that are not threatening.

I now know that I am one of these people who has spent a lifetime suffering and battling with an anxiety disorder. I have invested a year in therapy along with supplemental therapeutic treatments to understand and receive healing for it. I have learned that anxiety disorders are characterized by secrets. Shame keeps us from sharing our secrets and seeking treatment. I also learned, when I began my healing journey, that there are not a lot of books, particularly faith-based books, on anxiety. Most of what is available tends to be academic or medical resources, not for the average anxiety sufferer. At the beginning of my journey I really needed to hear the stories of other Christians who had struggled with an anxiety disorder, but I found this very hard to accomplish.

This book is a compilation of twenty-five years of journal writings, blog posts, notes from therapy, and lessons learned as God has taken me on a healing journey—specifically a healing from anxiety. God told me to share my message with others. You will read my original writings from different times in my life to see what I thought, how I felt, and what I prayed for during each time period. These writings will be labeled as journals or blogs.

I have also included my current perspective directly concerning these past journal writings and blogs. I consider this hindsight or lessons learned. Now that I am healed, I can explain my past with a fresher, clearer, and more mature understanding. Throughout this book, I share where I am in my healing journey, what God is teaching me, what I do when new issues arise, and some basic truths that I believe, if applied to your life, will completely change how you view yourself, God, and the world.

Reflection questions at the end of chapters are for those of you who would like to begin your own healing journey. Immediately following the questions, you will see a "Next Steps" section which provides some guidance that I recommend for you based on my experience. If you are reading this book in the hope of better understanding someone suffering from anxiety, then use the reflection questions or next steps as conversation starters.

Anxiety is a silent epidemic in our country that is on the rise and feeding our negative self-talk, addictions, inability to tell the truth, intimacy in relationships, and an overwhelming need to act like someone we are not in the hope of not being exposed. Please join me as I expose this demon. My prayer is that by sharing my experiences with anxiety, how I brought it to God for healing, and the resources that assisted me in my healing journey, you will connect in some way that encourages you to begin your own healing journey. Our stories matter, honesty matters, and divine intervention is real.

Here is my story.

Part 1 : The Awakening

For God has not given us a spirit of fear and timidity, but of power, love, and self-discipline.

2 Timothy 1:7 (NLT)

Chapter 1—I Am Not Okay

In July of 1990, I was eight years old and out of school for the summer. My mother who normally worked, had stayed home this particular day and had dropped me off at my friend's house while she ran errands. I never saw her again.

The next day, I remember my dad picking me up from my friend's house, and he had a nervous tension about him. I sensed his worry. He told me Mama had been in a car accident, and she was in the hospital. Of course, he assured me that everything was going to be okay, but I needed to spend the night with my grandmother while he went back to the hospital, but I would be able to see my mama soon. Three days passed while I waited at my grandmother's house and played with my cousins. I had not a worry in the world other than when I was going to be able to go to the hospital to see my mama. I knew she was going to be fine. We had been in a few fender benders before. No big deal. A life in which one of my parents didn't exist was incomprehensible to me. It didn't once cross my eight-year-old mind that something bad could happen.

After three days with my grandmother, I went to stay at my cousin's house. It was the middle of the night when my dad woke me up. Holding me, in the dark, with some of my family standing around, he whispered "Mama's gone to Heaven." I knew exactly what that meant. She was gone. I remember thinking so clearly to myself, "Everything is going to be fine, everything is going to be fine. We will be okay, you must be strong, your dad needs you."

This motto would replay in my mind for a significant part of my adult life. It would become what I told myself every time I felt like my world was crashing down on me, every time I felt weak, every time I felt scared, but mostly, every time I missed or needed my mother. I would eventually turn into someone who would not accept help, ask for help, or let on that I needed any help. These were never options in my mind. I was fine! Period.

But, I wasn't really, and thirty years later, I finally realized the lasting effects on me of my mother's traumatic death: the shock of her being there one day and not the next, the pain of a broken heart, the devastation of my family unit, the longing for my mother's touch, and the lies that the devil would begin putting into my thoughts. Eventually, I began to seek healing, letting down my guard to receive help. My healing journey led to the conversation with God shared below and the decision to write this book.

* * * * * * *

Journal Entry: A Talk with God about the Book

Me: *God what do you want this book to be about? What is your message?*

God: *Our talks. Your questions. Tell them all of it. It's all written down. I've given you a detailed memory. Open your journals, go back to those places, and share it. All the way up until now. That's what I want this book to be about.*

Me: *Um God. What? Like my diary journals? My prayers? My crazy thoughts and questions that I wrote in journals, so I wouldn't actually say them out loud? Lord, you know what's in there! Are you sure that's going to represent you well? I mean, you know how messed up I am, how confused, angry, sad and sometimes just down right mean I am. Lord, do I have to share the sad parts?*

God: *If you want to write My story Shellie, you share it all. Don't pick and choose the journals. Share it all or don't write anything with the expectation that it will be used to help others. For the last time, share it all. I am here.*

* * * * * * *

I had really planned for the pick and choose tactic to be an "out" on sharing everything. But with God's words in my mind, I was obedient. I started rounding up, pulling together, and trying to find all twenty-five years' worth of journals where I documented

2

my talks with God, my cries, my anger, my addictions and struggles, my pain, my secrets, my lessons learned, my revelations and circled Scripture and began forming it, with God's guidance, into this book.

I never thought God would ask me to share all of my personal writings. I never saw that one coming. I was thirteen when I started writing. It was therapy for me. My vocabulary grew as I progressed in my education, and my prayers got more specific and honest as I matured in my walk with God, but the premise of my writing was always the same—questions, curiosities, prayers. I was spending time talking with God before I even knew what quiet time with the Lord meant.

People have asked me how I spent so much time alone, and my answer is that I simply hung out with God and prayed and thought. Part of me always wondered if people thought I was weird for spending so much time alone. I definitely got mixed reactions when I told people that my alone time was actually my time with God. I could tell they thought it was a strange way to spend my time. But not God, He never made me feel weird. He was always there. He always answered my questions. He never shamed me for questioning anything and everything. So, I never felt uncomfortable asking Him anything and everything.

He let me ponder all sorts of things, small and big, generic and specific. Why are we here? Who is the devil? Why do painful things happen? Why did He choose green for the grass instead of pink or blue? Why did He decide to get rid of the dinosaurs? Do I get the same couple of angels my whole life as protection or does He change them up? Does my mom know I miss her and I am doing my best without her? Does He get tired of me asking so many questions?

And mostly, over and over, I would ask Him for as long as He kept me here, if I could work for Him somehow. I thought that I didn't act or look like those "proper" Christians—I sinned a LOT. I didn't even know all the sins, but I knew God. He'd always been there, and I loved Him. Could I work for Him in this life until it was time to go home?

The point is that my relationship with God continues to be made up of a lot of questions, and I'm thinking constantly. It's hard for me to ever shut my mind off. But, God just sits right there with me for hours on hours helping me ponder life, my pain, my struggles, and what I read in the Bible.

God wants me to share my writings which reflect my journey to help someone who might need them. I don't know everything God will do with this book. He will reveal it in His time. But, for now, I do know I am sharing how He took thirty years of confusion and pain and healed me from it. He saved me over and over again from the darkness of this world. If you are currently struggling to find healing and don't know where to begin addressing it all with God, I am sharing my experience. My hope is that you will see part of your life somewhere in my journey, and then, you will find God everywhere in your circumstances. Ultimately, I hope you will let Him walk you through your wounds, talk to you, and heal you.

Reflection Questions:

1) Have you experienced a traumatic or negative life-changing event at some point in your life? Examples could be a divorce, a death, an abusive relationship, bullying, neglect, a near-death experience, or anything that dramatically changed the trajectory of your life.

2) Did you receive healing from that event? How?

3) Do you suffer from extreme anxiety or post traumatic stress related to one or more of these events? If you are not sure, please take the time to research what anxiety or post traumatic stress looks like in someone's life.

Next Steps:

If you answered yes to questions one or three, this book is for you. It may be time to start thinking and praying about your own healing. Ask God to reveal any area that has negatively affected you, changed who you are, changed the way you react to and look at life, or any area where you may need His healing. Wrestle with this in prayer until He reveals areas He wants to heal in you.

Chapter 2—The Orphaned Lifestyle

There is a fire lit in a person who believes in healing from past issues. It is a God fire—a fire bigger than Hell, and when it is lit, the devil has no chance.

At the age of thirty-seven, I found myself in intensive therapy. I had never gone to a therapist before, and suddenly, I was going twice a week to two different therapists trying to unravel a life filled with anxiety. I will go into more detail later and explain how I got to a place to seek therapy. First, though, I think it is important to share a few things I learned in therapy and to take you back to the time of my mother's death when I was eight. That was when the anxiety actually showed up for the first time. Listed below are the exact issues that I was suffering from that brought on my anxiety and basically caused an identity crisis. The first column lists the root causes of some of my issues followed by the second column that lists the associated emotions or identities that the devil would eventually and subconsciously make my reality. These emotional labels or identities became open doors where the devil and his demons came in and changed how I saw myself, my reality of this world, my thinking, my emotions, and ultimately, how I reacted to circumstances.

Root Cause (Issue)	Emotional Labels or Identities (Open Doors)
Trauma	emotional trauma, shock, loss, victim
Orphan Lifestyle	motherless, displaced, searching, discontent, bound emotions
Abandonment	unprotected, betrayed, displaced, alone, emotionally abandoned
Anxiety	impatience, restlessness, stress, weariness, worry, addiction

Well, damn! This list was given to me by my counselor, and when I read it, it was like a ton of bricks literally knocked me in the face, heart, and soul. It was compiled from a questionnaire I took concerning my anxiety. The list was overwhelming for me to read and hard for me to process because first of all, it accurately pinpointed how I had journeyed through life, the way my thought process worked, and my insecurities. Secondly, until confronted with that list, I had never consciously thought that was how I acted or felt. I know that sounds odd, but it was and still is confusing to me that I didn't see any of these issues before meeting with my counselor the way it is laid out above.

You see, that's the nature of deception. The lies from the devil become truth until revealed as roadblocks to keep us from living a full life. Until exposed, lies exist for us as normalcy. We don't see them for what they are. THAT'S THE BIG SCHEME THAT DUPES US—THE FRAUDULENT NATURE OF DECEPTION. Scary is what it is, at first, but later, fear is followed by a huge sense of relief and a whole lot of tears when the devil's lies are exposed, and we can work free of them. For the first time in my ENTIRE life (all thirty-seven years), I felt a sense of hope that maybe I wasn't the problem and just maybe there was help now that I could see what was affecting me.

This idea of an orphaned lifestyle came up a lot when I started my therapy. I had never thought of myself falling into this category because although my mother had died, my dad had raised me. I wasn't completely parentless. However, the more I learned about it, the more I understood the nature of that lifestyle and how I was a part of the orphaned lifestyle club. My orphan mentality was very evident in one blog post I wrote a year before starting therapy, about what life was like without a mother.

* * * * * * *

Blog Post: Filling the Void
June 13, 2018

Most people that know me know I grew up without a mother for most of my life. She was hit by an eighteen wheeler when I was eight and passed three days later. Life would never be the same for my dad and me as we knew it. And we both would struggle to find our way again and carry on. So at age eight and thirty-three we began putting our foot one step in front of the other while picking up the pieces and trying our damn hardest to put them back together without falling off the deep end.

Life before mama passed was full of love, God, hard work, and singing. Oh, how she could sing! And she sang her heart out for God whenever she could in church, in the car, at other people's weddings, and at home while we cleaned. A funny memory I have is her singing to a country song and it cussed in the song and I said ooh mama you aren't supposed to cuss and she said baby you can if it's in a song. That still cracks me up today! She had all these cute ways about her that made her seem like a rebel and an angel all wrapped into one. But she loved people, her family, my dad, and me like no other. She truly was just a southern beam of life when she entered a room. I remember her mannerisms, voice, laugh, and quirks still to this day as if she left yesterday.

My parents and extended family on both sides are hard workers. We lived in a trailer while my dad and my mom basically hand built our first house. Mama was tough. Her mom was tougher! My mawmaw waited tables to provide for her 4 kids. My mawmaw lost both of her daughters about a year apart—my mom and my aunt. But, she kept going. She was just such a trooper. Looking back, I don't know how she did it.

My parents started dating in middle school. They got married at age seventeen and nineteen, and they were married sixteen years before she passed. Before she passed, we were happy, they were happy, and life was so good living in the country outside of Opelika, Alabama, riding four-wheelers with my cousins, hosting Christmas at our house for the family, going to church, and just living life in a small, protected bubble of love.

Then everything changed. Just like that, that life was over. And the void began. My dad didn't skip a beat on parenting. Through his pain and struggles he was always there for me and loved me like no other. We wouldn't really talk about her or what happened for about ten years. The memories were too raw and painful. We would only go there every once in a while and shed some tears together when one of us just couldn't avoid it. But, mostly we would cry separately in our rooms or wherever when no one was around. It was easier that way. Plus, it was a place where we could let God have it without being judged, I think. A place where we could be mad as hell and ask that question of why . . . why me, why her, why us?! But, it was also the place where God would always reassure us that she was well taken care of, we would see her again, and HE was going to carry us through. And HE did. But, the void was still there.

It took me a while to even understand the void. It was like a friend/enemy that walked around with me. It made me a soul searcher and an extremely reflective person that I don't think I was initially, other than my natural curious nature. That's the fun and interesting aspect of the void. It gives you a purpose. It's like you are constantly looking for whatever it is that's going to fill it. It's exhausting, liberating, full of let downs, and full of exciting surprises. And it makes for one hell of a good prayer life because I was in God's ear constantly trying to get clarity. HE was always available to listen and ready to guide the search.

I got a Philosophy degree trying to understand this void, life, God, and eternal life after this one. The degree helped, but the void was still there. I moved away from my hometown for ten years to continue my education, work, and try to find what it was that would fill the void. All of that was so freeing, being on my own in a different town, but the void travels with you. It eats away at your happiness because it was always quick to remind me that I would never feel love or happiness the way a mom makes you feel them, and then there is that whisper that the void uses to remind you that you are a little broken and there is no fixing you. Oh, the devil and his lies.

The void will tell you that other people know it too just by looking at you so insecurity arises that keeps you in your place by not letting you bloom or be the whole person God made you to be. Because there is a piece of your soul gone, not just from the death, but from the reality that people and happiness can be taken from you at any moment. So, the void keeps you from letting people in or loving wholeheartedly the way you want.

When things would feel too good for me, I would quietly take one step back from that happiness so I wouldn't get hurt. I kept my family at arm's length, my co-workers, my friends, and my relationships. I controlled how close people entered into my world because I wasn't going to give any opportunity for another void to develop. I knew I couldn't handle it. I used to think I was strong, because I could be somewhat unaffected by emotions or hardships that other people seemed to face, but now I see it as guarded and just living a portion of who God made me to be. There is no strength in that.

As I became older and my walk with God matured, I realized that fear of this beautiful life is not what my mom would have wanted for me. I was ready for marriage, kids, to be around my wonderful family again, so I moved home. Layer by layer I was peeling off my guarded shell and going after the things that scared me the most. But the void travels, remember. So, it was still there taunting me in the back of my mind. However, I was determined that God wanted more from and for me. So, that void was just gonna have to be on board while I went after my happiness. Moving home brought its own reminders of the pain because I ran into people constantly that knew and loved my mom. They would bring her up, I would smile, and then I would cry at night because I didn't want to relive it all again. No one knew her in Birmingham. It was safe there—no reminders of that part of my life.

And then I met my husband. I knew him as a child, but it had been years. And I tiptoed into falling in love with him. I wanted to go all in fast because I knew he was something special, that he was the man I was going to marry, but that broken piece of me wouldn't let me enjoy this happiness with open arms yet. Later we got married. The void was sitting there with me on the day of my wedding reminding me that loved ones can be taken from you. It took me a while to truly love Jeff the way he deserved because of my fear. But through my husband's patience and love for me, and with God's patience and love for me, I started to love and let myself be loved the way I had always wanted. The void was starting to get quieter. It was still there but not every day. And when it did show up, I kind of started giving it the finger and thanking God for my blessings, and that void in my heart showed up less and less.

Then I had my baby. There is not a void or pain or fear in this world that could stop me from screaming how much I loved him. And the bond that developed between my husband and me, because of that little guy, was something I never knew existed. People can tell you, but until you experience it for yourself no words can describe it.

* * * * * * *

I need to interrupt the blog here to explain its ending. At the time, I actually believed and felt what I wrote next. Marriage and having my son did bring some healing from losing my mom. But, I wasn't fully healed. That was just the beginning of my journey toward healing. Motherhood would later show me how much I was not yet healed. But, I think it's important to share how I felt in the moment for those who struggle with feeling a sense of healing, only later to find out that it was just one of the layers in their healing and there are many more to be peeled back. There was so much that God still needed to reveal to me. He is a gentle God. He knew the process would have been too much all at once. Here is how I ended the blog a year before I entered therapy.

* * * * * * *

So now I actually have the family life that I remember as a child. I am loved and in love. The void, fear, anger, and doubt don't really come around anymore. I've learned that surrendering to God's plan and HAPPINESS for your life can fill the void that the devil tries to create. I have no control over the future. I can't avoid tragedy or sickness or pain the way I wish I could. But, I can live and love in the moment, knowing that I am surrounded by blessings, and it's just selfish to not be grateful for those happy moments because of some bad ones. I plan to love my son, my husband, my family, my friends, the students I teach, my co-workers, and anyone else I meet with open arms and with everything I have, and the irony in that for me is that this has always been the remedy for killing my void.

* * * * * * *

Through the years, I would find myself circling a certain Scripture seeking identity. This search for identity was one of the early signs I showed of the orphaned lifestyle. I didn't have a mother to watch these qualities in real time, in action, functioning in the world.

I constantly looked at and obsessed over becoming the Proverbs 31 woman. I have notes in my journal that I focused on this Scripture in 2005, 2009, 2010, 2012, 2014, 2016, 2017, and in 2018. Below are some of the things I noted about her over the years.

* * * * * * *

Journal Entry: Proverbs 31 Woman

Everything she has to offer is valuable.
Her husband has full confidence in her; she brings him good not harm.
She works eagerly and vigorously.
She is always bringing goods.
She provides food for her family.
She buys land and plants.
She is strong.
She gets up early.
She trades for profit.
She uses her hands to work.
She is kind and giving to the needy.
She does not fear storms because she was prepared.
She makes coverings for her bed and wears fine clothes.
Her husband is respected in the city and associates with the elders.
She makes and sells stuff.
She has dignity and does not fear the days to come.
She speaks with wisdom and provides faithful instruction.
She is not idle.
Her children think she is blessed.
Her husband praises her.
Charm is deceptive and beauty is fleeting, but a woman of the Lord should be praised.
She should be honored and praised.

I have found myself going back and forth reading about the Proverbs 31 woman through the years trying to check myself against her example. See, that's the thing with an orphaned lifestyle—you don't have a parent or parents to use as a mirror for how to act, specifically for me that female parent. So, you grab hold of pieces of the puzzle of life that you believe to be true, that look right, or that look trustworthy. No matter how many times I read these verses, I have always felt really far from being that woman. But, I have never given up. Each year, I can see a little more of her becoming alive in me. I always smile to myself. God was and is teaching me how to be the woman He made me to be, even though I lost my mom—the woman who would have shaped my identity more than any other.

Reflection Questions:

1) Are there any open doors where the devil has slipped in and distorted your thinking? You may notice you have an open door if you find yourself more and more cynical, angry, skeptical, judgemental, sad, confused, or just less and less like your old self.

2) Do you feel like you are constantly trying to fill a void with things such as unhealthy relationships, addictions, work, or sadness? Do you ever feel like you actually fill the void or just create more chaos and misery in your life?

Next Steps:

Ask the Holy Spirit to search your heart and reveal any of these open doors. Then, ask the Holy Spirit to reveal biblical truths to you or guide you toward someone who can reveal the biblical truths.

Chapter 3—Finally Being Transparent

In 2017, I began writing a blog entitled *Divine Intervention*. This blog was the beginning of the sharing of my struggles, my thoughts and questions on life, and my pain with whoever was interested in reading it. I vowed to be completely transparent in the blog. In hindsight, it was just the beginning of God breaking me down to build me back up. I posted blogs for about two years, tip-toeing around my emotions with my readers until one conversation, one moment of divine intervention, caused a shift in the trajectory of my writing.

It started with a girls' night out with a best friend. We got on the topic of my blog, and she basically told me that I was not being honest. She said I was just writing the same story a lot of people write, so it was nothing unique, and I wasn't allowing myself to be vulnerable. At first, I was offended and didn't understand, but after I thought about it, I realized she meant that I wasn't sharing the actual painful details of my struggles. I was being too generic when I wrote about my life. I was sharing the lessons I'd learned, how I'm better now and grateful I had learned from those lessons, and how I wanted to share them with other people—but I never actually gave any intimate details. I wasn't letting people know how even though I had learned these lessons, I was still broken. I didn't know how to apply things I had learned, and I was embarrassed to ask for help or reveal too much to others. I was creating a facade through my writing that she didn't think was relatable to readers looking for raw truth.

She said something like, "You're not okay, even though you say you are, and you're not writing about that." She has been one of my best friends for almost thirty years, so she knew what she was talking about. We call each other soul sisters because we share our most intimate struggles with each other. We talk about God, our pain, our mistakes, our regrets, and we'd been doing this over wine for two decades.

We are both adults now, with marriages and children, so we don't get to have these precious, intimate conversations as much anymore. However, when we do, it is always raw and honest—a completely judgment-free zone. After our conversations, I feel refreshed. This friend believed in me as a writer when I wouldn't dare share my writings with anyone else. She knew that so far, I wasn't being completely honest, vulnerable, and real with my audience, and she told me it showed in the blog.

She had to leave soon after the conversation that evening. After she left, I went to the bathroom and cried to God. "Is it true God?" And then I knew, yeah it's true. I was way more broken than I thought or was willing to admit. The reality of this moment was one of the scariest times with God that I have ever had. The next blog I posted on May 6, 2019 continued the raw truth of what was really going on with me.

First though, before I share that blog, I need to give you a little background on what happened the night before I wrote that May 6th entry. My husband, son, and I had just left the Easter service at our church. I don't remember specifically what the sermon was about, but I remember my pastor saying, like he had said a million times before, "Give me one year. Go all in with God and our church for that one year and see how much your life changes."

I sat there wondering to myself, "After eleven years of attending the same church, why won't you go all in, Shellie?" Why would I only dabble in the things my church had to offer? I knew the answer automatically—I was broken. I had secrets, memories, and a past, and I didn't want to talk about any of those things. I didn't want them exposed. I could only hide them for so long from people, so I couldn't go all in. Just that reality, thinking about how much I was hiding, made me realize I needed help. I needed healing.

I cried the whole way home from church that night. When we got home, I looked at my husband and said, "I'm not okay, and I need some professional help. I can't do this on my own." He walked over, hugged me, and made me feel safe. I called my church for help the next day and wrote the blog entry you are about to read.

Blog Post: No, I'm Not Okay
May 6, 2019

I say I am. I want to be. I try to be. But, I'm not okay. I struggle with severe anxiety, worry, and fear. Not sometimes, but every day, around every person, in every situation, and mostly alone with my own thoughts. Even now, at this moment, writing this, I am full of anxiety about saying any of this out loud, about the people that will read it, about how it will make me look, about how it makes me feel weak. I hate feeling weak. I despise pity. But, I am so uncomfortable in my own skin that healing has to happen. I am thirty-seven, and I am only now fully admitting this to this extent. I've realized some of this about myself throughout the years, but the reality I'm facing now is so raw, and messy, and painful, and confusing, and scary that if it wasn't for my son and my husband, I would rather live in denial with the anxiety than do the work it's going to take to heal. I wouldn't wish this process on my worst enemy. It's that bad.

The anxieties (it is plural because there are multiple ways it shows up) that I live with make me fear every single situation. The typical situations that most people talk about feeling anxious about, like public speaking, before taking a test, job interviews, and other big events, are only a small portion of my experience with anxiety. Honestly, that's why I never realized I actually had a problem because it seems a lot of people struggle with anxious moments before these types of circumstances. But mine goes way beyond that. One aspect is that I am constantly in fear of what is going to happen next. I have an inability to live in the moment because I cannot stop thinking about the future. My mind has this need to prepare me for what is going to happen next or the worst case scenario. This tendency has ruined some of the most beautiful moments for me. I have really started to recognize this aspect of the worry in moments with my one year old. It's one of the main reasons I am choosing healing.

The fear shows up most before moments with people, all people, including my own family and closest friends. I really have to prepare myself to "act okay." Yes, I eventually settle in and enjoy myself, and laugh, share, play, talk, listen, and have fun. I am not a depressed person. I am not suicidal. I am full of hope and an eagerness to experience all God wants for me. That's a whole confusing angle in itself. My soul and the core of me love life, socializing, and being a part of things. I'm not sad all the time. I'm just constantly fighting a battle within myself. It's exhausting. A better word is debilitating. When I don't have the fight in me (to act normal), I withdraw, drink, or take a sleeping pill to just stop the process in my mind. I read my Bible, go to church, pray, do yoga, write, go for walks, or call a friend and try to be what they need. ALL of it, just to get out of my own head. It's a never ending cycle that is just so damn EXHAUSTING!

This cycle completely crushes potential. I love to do, and actually think I am decent at, so many different things. I am a learner and a sharer of my experiences. But, there are so many things I don't share or won't try or don't do because of my anxiety. I have fought the urge to clam up or isolate myself because I am strong willed (thank you, Jesus) and have a strong desire to experience all of what this life has to offer. My mother only got the chance to live life to the fullest for thirty-two years. I refuse to take this life for granted. I've always felt that way. I've put myself in situations that literally caused panic attacks, and I knew that they would, because I refused to give in to this stronghold on my life. But, it doesn't matter because it's always there. The anxiety goes wherever I go. Some days, months, or years I fight it better than other times, but I lose the battle a lot and hate myself for it.

Yes, this type of anxiety packs shame and guilt in its suitcase. As if the anxious moments or fear wasn't enough, after I feel like I made it through that moment, I get to wallow in the shame and guilt I feel for not following through with something I said I would do or go to. I self-medicate in a way I know is wrong, lash out at someone in anger because the anxiety got me so worked up, completely fall apart with someone and feel embarrassed afterwards, but mainly I feel the shame of how I represented myself as someone who knows and loves God so much but still struggles. The anxiety feeds the shame, which feeds the embarrassment, which feeds the guilt, which all feed the bad habits. It's a cycle, a never-

ending cycle. And when you think you have conquered it, gotten to the root of it, handed it over to God—another layer pops up that brings it all back. It literally starts to make you feel crazy, different, alone, desperate, confused, defeated, and scared. If it wasn't for prayer, people in my life that love me, and the power of the Holy Spirit whispering God's truths to me throughout the years, I don't know how I would have made it this long carrying this much weight.

I am sharing this for those who feel the same way. Our stories matter. Our testimonies matter. Our struggles and triumphs matter. There is healing, but there is also a process of healing, a point of refusing denial, a point of surrender and vulnerability that starts the process. I am there. It's a rocky road, but healing is under every rock I pick up and turn over and I'm ready to face the truth. I will share my process for those who want to join me on a journey of healing. It will be uncomfortable for me. I will cringe a little when I see people in public knowing they might have read my secrets. BUT, I will also smile and thank God for the healing process and any friends who may have joined me along the way.

* * * * * *

This was my turning point. My blog post about anxiety chronicles my attempt to expose the lies in my life. The lies that told me that I have to hide who I am and the way I feel. I needed to make the declarations in this post from May 6, 2019 publicly for ammunition to fuel what was to come, and to motivate or push me forward to healing. The post was me being completely honest, for the first time, about how anxiety affects me. I admitted the anxiety was that bad, and it had always been that bad. In the following months, I would begin intense counseling, soul searching, and spiritual warfare.

Reflection Questions:

1) Are there parts of your life that you are hiding from others, even your best friends or family? Why do you think you feel the need to hide them?

2) Are there parts of your life that you are even hiding from yourself? This would be events in your life, habits you have, or feelings that you refuse to revisit, sort through, or pray about. What are your "I'm not going there" topics?

3) What fears do you have that you feel the need to keep private?

Next Steps:

Baby steps lead to big steps. This is your chance to begin being vulnerable. Pick one of your fears, maybe one that has been around for a long time nagging at you, and find a trusted friend or family member with which to share this fear. Just saying it out loud is a huge next step. The feeling of release will be a weight lifted off of you. Also, this will give you the chance to listen to someone else's perspective on your fear. It will give you some material to bring to God in prayer. You can discuss with Him your understanding of your fear versus the perspective of your loved one, and even ask Him what He thinks.

Part 2: Exposing the Lies

Don't worry about anything; instead, pray about everything. Tell God what you need, and thank him for all he has done. Then you will experience God's peace, which exceeds anything we can understand. His peace will guard your hearts and minds as you live in Christ Jesus.

Phillipians 4:5-6

Chapter 4—Understanding Anxiety

In therapy, I was asked when I first noticed that my anxiety had shown up. I'd never thought about this before. That was the beginning of my really taking a look back to the time around my mom's death. I realized that the anxiety, or the devil's lies, entered very soon after she died.

Before she died, none of my crippling anxiety existed. I was brave, lighthearted, full of energy and laughter, a free and curious spirit who was confident in her life and her place in the world. I sang in front of the entire church multiple times, performed solo in talent shows, and had a big personality. I was definitely not shy or timid. I never questioned what I was going to say, if I was loved or wanted, and did not feel any pressure to be any other way than exactly how God made me. That is what I recall and what people of that time, my memories, and pictures tell me of my life up until age eight. Then, my mom was suddenly gone. It was a tragic accident, and everything changed. Anxiety showed up then.

Therapy helped me explore the different types of anxieties that I experienced at different moments in my life after her death. All my experiences were clouded with anxiety, debilitating worries and fears that would show up unannounced. However, fear came in various forms and was triggered by different circumstances. In order to understand what I needed to be healed from, I spent time in therapy identifying and labeling my different types of anxiety and the feelings and experiences tied to them.

I came up with the following list—this is what I shared with my therapist and church mentors. The numbered list has names I gave the different ways anxiety has shown up in my life. These are not clinical titles, but my way of developing a language to discuss my struggles with the people helping me.

1) Sickness Anxiety

The year or two after my mom died, I don't remember a lot. My memories now are blurry, but I know anxiety showed up (or the devil you might say) immediately. It showed up at age nine in the form of sleepless/restless nights, horrible stomach pains, and constant body aches. Later, in my years as a teacher, I realized this is how anxiety shows up in children. I had no idea at the time. I simply thought I was sick all the time.

It is God who arms me with strength and keeps my way secure.
2 Samuel 22:33 (NLT)

I can do all this through Him who gives me strength.
Philippians 4:13 (NLT)

2) Performance Anxiety

The next memories I have of anxiety showing up is at dance recitals as a child. All of a sudden, I went into complete panic mode when I got on stage to perform with my dance class. I was on the front row and couldn't remember a single step. This was devastating because I loved dancing. I knew those routines with my eyes closed. It was completely uncharacteristic of me to go numb, panic, and lose my grip on my reality. I watched others out of the corner of my eye and faked my way through it. I never told anyone about those moments on stage. This was the start of how I faked the way I acted to cover up what I was feeling.

By the beginning of my teenage years, my performance anxiety showed up anytime I went to perform in front of anyone for any reason, such as public speaking or singing. Eventually, singing in front of anyone became out of the question. The fear that hung over that anxiety was particularly disheartening because my mother had been a singer, and before her death, singing was a huge passion of mine as well. The devil stole my voice, my ability to perform, and my confidence that those things were a gift from God. This was the first potential the devil killed in me.

For He chose us in Him before the creation of the world to be holy and blameless in His sight.
Ephesians 1:4 (NLT)

No, In all these things we are more than conquerors through Him who loved us.

Romans 8:37 (NLT)

3) Relationship Anxiety

I have been in many ungodly and unhealthy relationships. I did not know my value. I would choose to date guys I knew I would never marry just because I didn't think the type of guy that I wanted to be with would love me when I was this broken. God proved that wrong by giving me my husband. I still struggle receiving love from him or showing him love the way I want because of the walls built up around my heart.

This anxiety about relationships originates from losing someone that I loved so much. Such a loss turns a part of your heart to stone. You don't even realize it when it happens, but you no longer feel love the way you used to. Even when you do feel it, you are suspicious of being vulnerable with anyone because when you opened yourself up before, you suffered a devastating loss. As a child, I loved my mom with a childlike trust that believed nothing could take her from me. After all, what child thinks their parents won't always be around? But, then I lost my mom in the accident and for that relationship to disappear (because that's what it felt like as a kid, like she disappeared), it broke my trust in believing that love was a real thing. I'm pretty sure it did this to my dad, too. I still loved people, but with a heart that didn't go all in, trust, or easily receive love from others. God eventually healed this in me, but first, I had to admit the reality of my heart's condition, and no one wants to admit that they have a heart of stone.

"Never will I leave you; never will I forsake you."

Hebrews 13:5 (NLT)

"...for I am the Lord, who heals you."

Exodus 15:26 (NLT)

He heals the brokenhearted and binds up their wounds.

Psalm 147:3 (NLT)

4) Belonging Anxiety

Anxiety kept me from feeling like I had a place among "church people" for a good part of my life, up until about ten years ago when I started going to Church of the Highlands (Highlands). Highlands and their way of sharing God's love for His people rescued me and brought me back to the truth. This stronghold was not completely broken just because of my wonderful church community. I'd been going there for eleven years and only recently chose to go "all in," as Pastor Chris Hodges calls it, because I had never wanted to reveal all that I am sharing in this book. Up until going "all in," I still didn't think I was worthy of God's love or that I would be accepted if I revealed how broken I was.

If God is for us, who can be against us?

Romans 8:3 (NLT)

Even when I walk through the darkest valley, I will not be afraid, for you are close beside me. Your rod and your staff protect and comfort me.

Psalms 23:4 (NLT)

5) Physical Anxiety

This particular anxiety creates a physical reaction that is the opposite from relaxed, calm, joyful, patient, or what one might consider a normal, under-control feeling. It literally creates panic. My heart races. I can't catch my breath, I'm nauseous, and long for something to calm these feelings. This is where the addictions show up looking like a knight in shining armor to provide a release, a distraction, a strategy (crutch) to control the anxiety. The saving grace for worry, fear, and anxiousness showed up in my early adult life as withdrawal from people and social situations, and alcohol and cigarette addictions. Huge lies about who I was and my purpose here on earth would be dictated by these addictions for many years to come.

And the peace of God, which transcends all understanding, will guard your hearts and your minds in Christ Jesus.
Philippians 4:7 (NLT)

6) Overachieving Anxiety:

The lie behind this anxiety is that my self worth is directly related to my accomplishments. This one can show up as pride—if I can accomplish something, I can prove that I am not broken. The thought process behind this anxiety is that broken, hurt, or emotionally unstable people are not capable of doing well in life. Therefore, if I am successful, then I must not be broken, hurt, or emotionally unstable. Success is different for every person, but when I was driven by my need to overachieve, it meant always having a good work ethic, achieving my higher education goals, and being independent. If I am independent, accumulate many college degrees, and do well at my job, then the anxiety is not winning, my past has not scarred me, and I am just fine. Hiding behind my busy schedule and my accomplishments allowed me to avoid my pain and hope that others would not know there was anything wrong. Ultimately, the more I accomplished, the more my pride in myself grew. I became mainly dependent on my own ability to succeed and less dependent on God. It wouldn't surprise me if I even came across as arrogant to some.

Do nothing out of selfish ambition or vain conceit. Rather, in humility value others above yourselves.
Philippians 2:3 (NLT)

7) Control Anxiety

This anxiety requires my attention and ultimately affects my relationships. It steals from my day-to-day life. It requires me to keep tabs on the level at which the anxiety might show up, hence urgently needing my attention and control. It makes me misdirect blame on others when I feel uncomfortable or my emotions seem out of my control. It keeps me from the true intimacy that God intended for marriage and other relationships. Moreover, it keeps me from the intimate relationship that He wants to have with me.

When I feel out of control with my emotions, I withdraw to find my safe zone, alone with God, where I feel in control of the anxiety. The anxiety about losing control might just be the deepest of them all. Its roots are buried under layers of lies. The need for control is my biggest weakness, but until I went all in, I mistakenly believed it was my greatest strength. Control meant power, stability, and discipline, which are all strengths, so my thought process was if I am in control, I am strong. Isn't that crazy? What an oxymoron. Control is the number one lie that will keep us distant from God and His purpose for our lives. I had to hand over control to Him in order to be transformed, healed, and changed. It just took me about thirty years to even begin to unravel this one. I am still a work in progress in this area, for sure!

Therefore, whoever takes the lowly position of this child is the greatest in the kingdom of Heaven.

Matthew 18:4 (NLT)

For those who exalt themselves will be humbled, and those who humble themselves will be exalted.

Matthew 23:12 (NLT)

Now, looking back, I realize so many of my prayers weren't answered because my pride kept me from being honest with myself, with those in my life, and ultimately, with God. From my experience, God only answers my authentic and honest prayers. If my prayers are arrogant or self serving, He seems to ignore them, or He lets me take control of my life and pursue my selfish desire if I insist. The latter usually doesn't end well for me.

Following my selfish ambition has only gotten me off the path He planned for me, and I ultimately have ended up on my knees weak and needing His guidance because my life is spiraling out of control. Note, I don't mean my life is spiraling out of His control, but my control because I thought I knew what was best for me and didn't want His help. I tried taking control of my own life many times before. I have finally realized that's not how God works. I don't get to take the credit for my accomplishments and get His blessings at the same time. How would He be glorified unless He gets the credit? No, all of my accomplishments are directly because of His grace, divine intervention, and planned purpose for my life.

Reflection Questions:

1) Do you suffer from any of the above descriptions of anxieties to a level that you feel disrupts your life in a negative way? List the ones that you identify with.

2) When did you notice the particular anxiety or anxieties you listed in the previous question entering your world? Were there any traumatic events or major life changes happening during this time? Look back at the answers you gave for the Chapter One questions to connect any of those events to any anxiety you may be experiencing.

Next Steps:

Reread the Scriptures under any particular anxieties I listed that you also struggle with and meditate on the Lord's Word. Write the verse on a note card, and put it somewhere you can reread it daily until it starts to become your new truth. If you are unsure if your anxiety is linked to a lie (which they all are) or maybe you are not quite sure what lie you are believing, find someone in your life who knows Scripture and can help you identify the lie and replace it with a scriptural truth. This was actually a struggle of mine at first—I didn't know enough Scripture to replace the lies I was believing. Learning God's Word and committing it to memory is definitely part of the healing process.

Chapter 5—Finding Healing: Opening Pandora's Box

I had always heard the saying about opening Pandora's Box. Intellectually I understood the reference but I wasn't quite sure what it meant, and I didn't care- until it happened to me.

Before the box is opened, it lies dormant, but not completely hidden. You are always aware that it is there. Honestly, I always knew I had this box tucked away in me packed with memories, and the bad things of the past I didn't want to think about or relive. For most people, that box stays tucked away until a certain circumstance impacts them, a life event (good or bad)—a heartbreak, a failure, an accomplishment—and then that real emotion surfaces. At that point the box starts floating around, reminding you that it still exists, tempting you to open it and relive what is inside of it. It taunts and teases you with what lies within it. Mostly, it reminds you that it is there to be opened.

Anyone who suffers from PTSD, addictions, abuse, or any past trauma can probably relate to the scenario I'm trying to paint. The box floats at Christmas, marriages, funerals, relapses, successful and painful moments, and high and low moments. It floats to remind you that when you are happy, you shouldn't be because that box is full of "stuff" to remind you that you are not worthy of any peace and happiness. It floats when you are sad as a reminder that everything is worse than you think. Really, it is the devil and his taunting. The fear of opening the box is his tactic. The truth is that opening the box leads to healing but you just have to open the box! Admittedly, opening the box is going to feel like jumping into a fire knowing it will burn you alive, but have faith because the truth is you will come out brand new without a hint of ash. It's scary but worth it.

I knew when I started my journey of complete healing, that God wanted me to open my box of memories, fears, pain, trauma, and brokenness. I had to go back and revisit that little girl who was so scared, vulnerable, and confused.

The following blog post has writings from when I was in therapy and beginning to understand that I needed to open the box and work through my past. I hope that my writing will reflect how gentle God was with me through the process of examining my past. Because, let me tell you, opening that box is a process. It takes relying completely on God, and going through the box doesn't happen all at once, either. God is a good God for He only gives us what we can handle a little at a time. I'm so grateful for that because this part of my healing journey was probably the most difficult. I had spent an ENTIRE LIFETIME dodging, ignoring, drinking away, masking what was in the box. I knew the process wasn't going to be easy.

* * * * * *

Blog Post: My Journey Toward Healing . . .
Peeling Back the Layers
June 5, 2019

I previously wrote a blog about anxiety—the struggle with fear and worries that I live with—and I gave it a name. Anxiety is the clinical name for the way I feel on a day-to-day basis in most of my life experiences. Anxiety is a stronghold in my life and I wrote about it. Then, I began my search for healing, not for fixers, bandaids, excuses, or my typical denial technique (which is to accomplish something challenging or seemingly important, so that I can convince myself that I am fine and actually don't need any help at all), but true healing. God's healing. The kind of healing that doesn't just take the anxiety away for a time, but removes it completely, creating a new, clean slate, and making me new. I am believing in 100% healing. The moment I gave my stronghold a name was the moment I realized it actually did exist in me, in my everyday life. It was the day that I knew and admitted I needed help with this struggle, and I was desperate for healing. That was about a month ago. Here is my JOURNEY since then.

The healing journey became the process by which I would solve my equation, actually the process by which God would solve my equation. My equation was:

Pain + Covering up *(the boxed up past and emotions)* = **Anxiety**

That was all I knew. That is what I presented to God in a broken and scared state. Then, as He does, He immediately responded with a quiet whisper, "We have work to do, my child, but we must go back." It was something along those lines, and I buckled over weeping because I knew what that meant. My initial response was, "No, please, no! I don't want to go back there. Can we please just start from here and now?" But, I already knew I had to go back. Back to where the pain started, back to the event that changed my world, back to the tragedy of losing my mom.

I was confused by this because I had already healed from losing her. Her death had been thirty years ago. The majority of my life had been without her. The pain of her not being around is mostly minimal at this point and only shows up roaring loudly on certain occasions. I talk about her often and have very fond memories. My journey "back" was actually back to the little girl that was devastated by that tragedy. The little girl that didn't receive the healing that she didn't even know she needed. The little girl that began to shut down and build walls around her heart. The little girl that became capable of loving others and making sure they were alright, but incapable of truly receiving love from others. The little girl that crawled into the shell of her own scared, hurt, and confused emotions and became comfortable hiding there. Back to that little girl is exactly where God wanted me to go and exactly where I didn't want to go! But, I did because I wanted healing, and God's timing is perfect. He whispered, "It's time. I knew this day would come. You have the strength and joy of the husband and son I gave you . . . WE can do this now." God is so good! I understood it was time.

You see, I wasn't born with this anxiety-ridden, fearful nature. It developed and was created in me over time by the burying and ignoring and refusing to relive a tragedy. AND, I had become so accustomed to this way of being that I had absolutely no idea where to start for healing, what to pray to God about, or how to distinguish lies from truth. The lies, fears, doubt, pain, and worry had been there for so long that I liked them to a certain extent. They were how I was used to feeling and the possible absence of them was even scarier (if that makes any sense). The point here is that I needed additional help to peel back the layers—help beyond all the "self-help" books, meditation in Scripture, prayer, or the wine nights with friends talking about our secrets. I needed other people of faith to help me navigate this landscape. I couldn't trust my own self-talk or emotions anymore. I had done that long enough. It didn't work, but just pushed everything down deeper, buried everything lower, with walls built around every layer. This hot mess of hidden lies and feelings needed some professional help! So, I called my church, set up an appointment with a mentor, and I set up an appointment with a Licensed Professional Counselor. Why not get two therapists?! I was already in the midst of my reality, that healing must come, and I needed help with that. I was grateful to accept as much help as needed. And that's what I have been doing. Meeting with fantastic women of God, letting them unravel all of my buried pain, and doing my own private and personal walk with God, Scripture, and prayer.

I'm just at the beginning of this healing journey. Layers of pain, confusion, and unresolved emotions are being revealed and prayed over, and healing is coming. God is holding my hand and handling me gently, reminding me that I am still a child in His eyes, and I am letting Him hold me tight and walk with me one step at a time. It's a long overdue process, and I am enjoying it most of the time. I am committed and believing in true healing.

I originally wrote my May 6th blog on anxiety to share my story out loud with others. I was breaking down the first wall of fear by saying my struggle out loud. But, so many of you texted, messaged, and responded in one way or the other with your own "me too" stories of your struggle with anxiety. Thank you for that! First, because it made me feel less crazy and vulnerable. But, secondly it made me feel loved and reminded me why I share my story. Our stories matter!

Here is my takeaway as of this point in this journey: Our experiences as children, what happens to us and around us—the things that happen that are completely NOT our fault—travel with us as baggage into our adulthood if not dealt with properly early on. These circumstances shape us and become what we identify with, how we approach the world, how we interact with people, or how we withdraw. Negative life events change us from whom God intended us to be. If we recognize that we may have unfinished business from our past that we've brought along without even realizing it, we may also notice that it will kill or lessen our potential and show up as anxiety.

This is just my story and my experience. I only know what I'm learning, what God is so generously and gently teaching me. I truly believe there is healing from these layers of baggage and our slate can be wiped clean. We only have to lean in and do the hard work, go back to the places we thought we left behind, and trust with faith that Jesus truly set us free that day on the cross. We have to trust that the Son of God is at the Father's right hand in Heaven interceding in prayer on our behalf and ready to reveal His plan for healing in our lives as soon as we are ready to confess our true struggles, anger, pain, and confusion. This is where I am on my journey of healing. I am definitely at the beginning, but I now see a future where anxiety does not show up as my unwanted "companion" on a daily basis. I look forward to that day! It's already showing up less as I write this. I am not scared to share this. I am honored that I serve a healing God and I am expectant of His healing.

* * * * * * *

In the blog post I explain the "box" from my past in a few ways, such as layers to be unraveled, something buried, things covered up, a suitcase or baggage, etc. These metaphors all refer to some type of pain but are different ways of explaining what it felt like to deal with it through the years. Below are some of the items in the "box" from my past, the questions, feelings, memories, and moments that I needed to be healed from as recorded in a journal I kept during the healing process.

Once the box was opened, I realized there were categories or a patterned way of grouping the memories, pain, and questions. One category, for example, for me was, "What I Lost," and it wasn't much fun to go through. However, there are reasons for these categories or the pattern in which the items in the box are grouped together. The box is very well organized. God is not a God of confusion. Here were some of my categories:

Journal: Categories In My 'Box'

Questions:

• *Why do I need others' approval? Why do I never feel good enough or accepted?*
• *Why am I so nervous and uncomfortable around almost everyone? Why am I so uncomfortable in my own skin?*
• *How can I leave the most powerful experience with God and go straight back to feeling empty, weak, and unworthy? It's like the chains just won't completely break.*
• *I feel my best in the presence of the Lord, but I won't continue to seek Him everyday. Why won't I continue to put Him first?*
• *Why won't I go all in with you God?*

What I lost when I lost my mother:

• *A best friend*
• *Someone to take me to church, teach me about God, teach me how to be a woman, mom, daughter, and friend*
• *A place to be emotional, weak, helpless*
• *Someone to ask my girl questions to and a place to be vulnerable*
• *Someone I can be silly with, laugh with, cry with, PRAY with*
• *A role model I trust and respect*
• *The person I was made like*
• *The person I would sing with (I only sing alone now and cry when it sounds like her)*
• *My son's grandmother*
• *My mom at my wedding, when I graduated college, when I was pregnant, her presence when I was so scared during labor*
• *Someone to help me understand my dad and how to take care of him*
• *Someone to fight for me and protect me*
• *My childhood, my family, the three of us, my happiness in some way*

Journal Entry: Talks with God

God: *You can not have one foot in the world and one foot in our relationship.*

Me: *What would it be like if we were so close to the Lord that every decision we made felt like it was done in His presence?*

God: *Don't wish your life away. Be fulfilled in Jesus in the season you are in. The tasks I have for you in this season will prepare you for the tasks I have for you in the next season. Draw near to a godly woman who is already in the next season and learn from her so you are prepared for the next season. Be present in the current season.*

Me: *I need to find a godly female mentor who is older than me! I should pray for this.*

* * * * * *

These are how my talks with God often take place. I've never really dissected my talks with God until writing this book. I would just write them down or talk with Him through prayer. He prompts my thinking with Scripture, biblical truths, guidance on what steps to take next, and sometimes with a question. Then, I have an inner talk with myself, restating what God said in my own voice. It's my way of taking ownership of the thought God gave me and giving value to His voice because if I don't restate the thought, I can soon move on to something else. The Holy Spirit whispers - He doesn't scream or demand our attention. Many times God speaks to me, and I don't take the time to listen. I can also overpower His presence with my own thinking or the general distractions of life, and the thoughts He gives me slip away.

When God gives me instructions that I'm not ready to listen to, don't understand, or refuse to acknowledge because, like a child, I don't like what He's asking me to do, they form a category of their own in the box. God never changes, He does not make mistakes, and He does not tell us anything that isn't *important or that He* will allow us to dismiss. So, His directions will sit there in that box until we either are ready to carry out the instructions, or I believe, He eventually makes the ones we refuse to listen to part of our one-on-one conversation with Him when we get to Heaven. I imagine it will sound something like, "Daughter I'm so sorry you felt that pain. There were a few instructions I gave you hoping they would guide you away from that pain and allow you to reach your full potential, calling, and purpose." I don't imagine this to be in a scolding tone, but a reminder that He is the Father, He knows best, and the conversation in Heaven will be to reassure us of these truths—much like the conversations I believe my husband and I will have with our children when they avoid our instructions or guidance.

It's a good point to make here that prayer is not just when we go to God with our plans, thanks, needs, and fears. I mean that is prayer, too, but God is always present in our thoughts listening and responding if we would just start to differentiate His voice from ours. His voice comes as the thoughts and revelations that precede or prompt our thoughts and questions. He's always there, ready to guide us when we ask. We can even just sit silently and listen to Him. He says in Psalm 46:1, "Be still and know that I am God." A discipline I am not good at, but learning to do more, is just sitting and listening to what He wants to tell me. When I choose to shut my brain off and my mouth up and listen to what He wants to talk about, He's always ready to reveal the next step He has for me. Go figure. God has stuff to say that we didn't even know we wanted or needed to hear.

Reflection Questions:

1) What memories, emotions, experiences, or thoughts are in your box that you refuse to revisit or deal with? They may be topics you refuse to talk about with anyone or get defensive about if someone brings them up. You will know these because they may show up from time to time and affect you in some negative way. For instance, they may show up around the holidays or a certain season or date of the year. They may show up as overreactions you have to anything that reminds you of them or triggers you to think about them. They may show up when you listen to certain music or go to a certain place. Pay attention to any time you feel uncomfortable because you are reminded of the past and you immediately change the subject or even wallow in the pain.

Next Steps:

These areas you thought above are those that you need healing from. It is a process that may require some professional help to go through. This may be when you want to consider finding a trusted friend or family member, a counselor, therapist, or an older, experienced mentor to help you go through your box, little by little so that it is not too overwhelming.

Furthermore, it is important here to invite God into the process. He needs to know that you are not trying to heal yourself or believing that anyone else can heal you. He needs to know He is wanted and needed for healing. He is a jealous God, but He will not impose in areas He is not wanted. You are welcome to try this without God, but my belief and experience is that it will not work. You will not have the insight and emotional stability to complete the process fully, and no one person, other than God, will be able to give you all that you will need for complete healing.

Even if just acknowledging to God that you have a box from your past you need to deal with is all you are comfortable doing at this point, God will be so proud that you made this first step. He will be waiting when you are ready to move forward.

Chapter 6—Talks with Jesus

I will share two specific ways I learned to spend time with Jesus that were revolutionary for my healing process. I wrote down in my journal our intimate conversations, what I asked Him, His responses, and the lessons I learned from these conversations. I had never talked with Jesus like that in the past. I did not realize the power that these conversations would unlock in me—Jesus's power—that is available to us when we have His Spirit within us.

These specific ways of asking Jesus questions, sharing my emotions, and inviting Jesus into my memories and moments of pain opened up a vulnerability I had never had in prayer before. These conversations revealed how God had never left my side throughout the years, for even one moment. I hope that whoever reads these intimate conversations will get a glimpse of how precious our time is with the Lord, how powerful handing over our pain to Him can be, and how willing He is to talk back if we just give Him the time and honesty that any intimate conversation requires. After reading this chapter, try using these strategies on your own when you have conversations with Jesus, and I know they will help you also.

Strategy 1: Sharing Your Feelings with Jesus

This first strategy was given to me by my therapist and required me to write down any feeling I was having right in the moment as I was writing. For example, when I started to journal I would write if I was feeling discouraged, sad, happy, excited, angry, etc., and I would write this feeling down even if I didn't know why I was feeling that way at that moment. My therapist shared a tool with me—the *Feelings Wheel*. There are many versions of this online if you want to Google "Feelings Wheel."

The wheel is not essentially a Christian therapy tool and can be used in many types of therapy. However, my therapist knew that I wanted my therapy to be based on Scripture, biblical truths, and prayer, so she gave me a specific way to use it that involved identifying my feelings with the wheel and praying through them. The wheel starts with generic feelings in the center and gets more and more specific as you work your way outward. The point is that you can start with a simple emotion and get more specific with your feelings using the wheel to accurately express yourself.

You are supposed to write down this process of moving toward the outer edge of the wheel as it happens for journaling purposes. Even if you are not someone who typically journals, jotting down a few notes to record your thoughts as you work through the wheel can be very helpful. Once you have located the feelings from the wheel, bring them to Jesus in prayer, ask Him if He ever felt any of those feelings or emotions while He was here on Earth, then sit and wait for His response. Below, I have written in more detail how the process actually unfolds by walking you through an example of how I used the wheel.

I initially put off using the *Feelings Wheel* for a few weeks after it was given to me by my therapist. I was skeptical. Unfortunately, I also had very little patience, and I made the excuse that I didn't have time. The thought of just sitting around waiting for Jesus to speak to me seemed overwhelming and time consuming. How ridiculous that sounds now. How in the world do we make time for everything else in our lives, but can't give the Creator and Savior of the world an hour? Also, how do we constantly go to God with all our plans, thoughts, thank yous, prayer requests, and problems, but never find time to just sit and let Him say what He needs to say to us? Well, I was about to learn what I had been missing in my prayer life.

Here are the steps in detail recommended to me by my therapist for how I should use the *Feelings Wheel*:

Step One: Focus on a specific moment, a specific event, or any emotions that you have been struggling with lately or right now in the moment. Starting at the center of the wheel, identify the emotions that you are feeling and work your way outward, recording your more specific emotions as you go.

Step Two: Write a sentence about each emotion and how that emotion is making you feel or coming out in your actions and behaviors.

Step Three: Pick one of the emotions you wrote about. Ask Jesus this question, "Jesus, did you ever feel this way when you were here as a human on Earth?" Then, take the time to sit in His presence, listen for His answer, and write it down.

The sitting and waiting part of step three, for me, takes at least fifteen minutes or longer before I hear God respond. It takes me about that long to get my mind in reflection mode, quiet my own thoughts about my day or my problems, and come to Him with a clean slate. It is important that my mind is clear and ready to receive any answers or insights He has to offer after I have asked the question. Once I am totally focused on my time with Jesus, the process of hearing Him goes much quicker as I repeat steps one through three for each emotion.

Step Four: For the same emotion in Step Three, ask, "Jesus, do you want to say anything else to me about this emotion?" Then, take the time to just sit in His presence, as you did in Step Three, and listen to His answer. Write down His reply.

Step Five: Repeat this process for all of your emotions listed in Step One and explored more in Step Two.

Step Six: Finish the experience by responding back to God concerning what He said to you. This step is done at the very end after every emotion that you wrote down has been shared with Jesus (Steps One through Five). This is the end of the process. Respond to Jesus in whatever way feels natural for you.

Your response back to Jesus can take many forms:
• You can write down a few sentences that you feel you want to say back to God based on His responses.
• You may say it out loud to Him in prayer.
• You can draw a picture of what you are feeling after the time with God.

• You might want to sit and listen to worship music and praise Him as a response.

Do whatever feels natural for you and know that it may be different each time you try this activity.

Below is word-for-word what I wrote down one day while doing Steps One through Six. I recorded what I said to Jesus and what I heard from Him in the form of thoughts as I sat in His presence waiting for His responses. God talks to me in the form of pictures (visuals, visions of words, or scenes) and thoughts. I am also very reflective by nature, and at this point I can usually discern the difference between my own pondering and thought process as opposed to the thoughts or words from the Lord. There was no doubt that the Lord was responding to me throughout this activity because almost everything He told me was a new insight to me. I believed the complete opposite of what He was telling me before this activity and I did not have the background knowledge to come up with these realizations on my own. That's what made this experience so life changing and authentic for me. As I stated previously, I was initially skeptical about this process. Over time, it was conversations with the Lord, like the one below, that broke my chains. He corrected lies I believed with His truth, and He related to my human experience, counseled me, fathered me, and ultimately gently healed me.

Journal: Feelings Wheel Activity

Step One:
Emotions I am feeling (chosen from the Feelings Wheel):
Mad, Angry, Critical, Distant, and Skeptical

Step Two-Five:
Statements I wrote for each chosen emotion and Jesus's response:

1) Mad
I am mad that I am still dealing with the pain of losing my mom thirty years later.

His response:

I spent thirty years fighting the same battle, sharing the good news about our Father, only to be denied by my own people in my own hometown. One of my closest friends turned me over to be crucified after watching me spend my life sharing the truth. (Luke 22)

What He wanted to say to me or the lesson He wanted me to learn:

I loved my friend anyway. I knew I was going to die for all of the sins of the world, and I still continued. Your battle and time spent is not going unnoticed by Me. I've always been there making the way for you, just like I was there all those years ago in your bedroom when you would cry out to me. Don't be mad. This is the life I knew you would live. None of it is surprising to me. You don't understand now, but one day, you will. I am here. Keep doing the work.

2) Angry

I am angry that I didn't realize I needed to deal with my past or get help earlier.

His response:

I was angry in the marketplace. (Matthew 21:12)

What He wanted to say to me or the lesson He wanted me to learn:

It's okay to be angry. It is a natural emotion and a response to evil. I gave you that emotion.

3) Critical

I am critical of the adults that were around me when I was younger and their lack of realizing or noticing the impact their actions had and would have on me.

His response:

I was bothered by the men being hypocrites to the adulterous woman when I told them, "All right, but let the one who has never sinned throw the first stone!" (John 8:7 NLT) She was my child too.

What He wanted to say to me or the lesson He wanted me to learn:

The adults around you when you were young did the best they could at the time. Your battle is not with human flesh, but with demons of this world. (Ephesians 6:12)

Be critical of the evil that put blinders on their eyes so they couldn't see your pain. Criticize the devil and fight him with spiritual warfare. Remember, the battle is already won. And, I was there when you were young; I never left you. I saw your pain. And, My timing is perfect.

4) Mad and Critical

I am mad at and critical of myself for not being more honest about my struggles with anxiety and my past.

His response:

I felt that feeling when I couldn't tell Peter he was the denier and Judas that he was the betrayer. But, it wasn't the right time. It was hard for me to not offer the truth that I knew at that moment.

What He wanted to say to me or the lesson He wanted me to learn:

You can't be honest with what you don't know. You didn't have the insight you needed at the time to be honest about your struggles. The devil has his way in this world, and he blinded you from knowing that you needed to reach out and get help. You didn't know the impact not reaching out for help would have on you in the future. But, I did and that is why I was always there to listen and whisper truths along the way. I knew the day would come when you would recognize the role the devil had in your life and how he uses anxiety, guilt, confusion, fear, and shame to keep you from seeking help for your struggles. I knew the day would come when we would have this talk. Remember, I do all things for good, in My timing. The battle is already won.

5) Critical and Skeptical

I am skeptical that I will be healed and critical of myself for not trusting God more in any area that I need healing and to believe His promises.

His response:

Remember when I asked God to take my cup from me, if it was His will, the night before I was crucified? I was scared. You are just scared. But remember fear is not from me, but self-discipline, power, and love are all from me. (2 Timothy 1:7, Luke 22:42)

What He wanted to say to me or the lesson He wanted me to learn:

We have to change your thoughts, reveal the lies, and replace them with My truth. This will take time. Have faith. Be patient. Let me heal you. And then, you will see Me for who I really am and then you will see you for who you truly are, who I made you to be. The person I made you to be is amazing. You will like her. People will want to be around you, and you will want to be around them. You are My child. I chose you. You are perfectly made in my image and you are special to me. I am proud of you for doing this work. I have great plans for you to prosper, serve, and share Me through just being you.

6) Skeptical

I am confused about my feelings toward my past and skeptical about which of them are real and which are lies.

His response:

I was tempted and lied to for forty days by the devil in the wilderness. I understand this confusion and skepticism very well. (Matthew 4: 1-11)

What He wanted to say to me or the lesson He wanted me to learn:

When I was tempted, I used the words of the Father to fight the lies, and you will need to do that too. That is what the Living Word means. There is power in My words. I gave them to you to use just for this. Confusion is not from me. There is your first lie you have fought. Fight evil with good, lies with truth, sin with love, flesh with spirit. This is a discipline you will have to develop over time with practice and prayer. You cannot do this on your own. I think you know that now. You must seek Me and My words daily for this to be effective. I set it up that way. I am a jealous God for you. I want a relationship with you. I made you. You are my child. It brings me great pleasure to counsel you and share my truth. I love you. You understand this more now because I gave you Grayson, your son. You want the same things for him that I want for you. Teach him this young, and he will carry it. Your therapist will help you with this process too. I chose her for you. You are not alone.

Below is what I wrote as my final response to Jesus (Step Six). It was hard for me to put into words what I couldn't express because I was overwhelmed with emotion and gratitude for the responses Jesus gave me through this experience.

Step Six:

My final response to the Lord:

The Spirit talks within me. I am filled with emotion, not words. I don't know how to express what I'm feeling in words. The closest word I can find to use about how I feel is connection. It's something like that. Even though I don't have the words to express the emotions I am feeling toward what You have told me through this experience, I still hear you, and I understand the language of gratitude that my spirit is speaking. Thank you. One wall just fell, and I want more of this time with You, more of Your insight, more truths to replace the lies. This experience was not scary like I thought it was going to be; it was beautiful. This experience reminded me what it's like to be completely in Your presence, I am reminded that I'm Yours.

* * * * * * *

I have used this first strategy, sharing my feelings with Jesus, many times with very similar results. I write them all down in my journal. I enjoy going back and reading my journals when I need to be reminded of any truths that He spoke to me through each experience. The one that I just shared is the first experience I had with this strategy and I feel that it adequately shares the importance and intimacy of the strategy. I hope you see how healing and informative this process can be. It is a discipline that requires the time to sit in the presence of the Lord.

It could be beneficial to do once a week or once a month. First, it helps me check my emotions. By this I mean I actually have to become aware of what emotions I'm feeling at the moment. It doesn't matter for what reason I'm feeling them, but I need to give them a name and hand them over to Jesus. Next, I get to have a conversation with Jesus about His time on earth, how I feel, and why I feel that way. This makes the human aspect of the Trinity real for me. I have someone with which I can more easily connect. It reminds me that He really does know how we feel because He experienced our pains, struggles, and emotions just so He could have these intimate talks with us—so beautiful. Finally, I get to hear His thoughts regardless of my emotions. It is such an intimate experience and the best conversation you will ever have, I guarantee!

Strategy 2: Inviting Jesus into Your Memories

The other activity that I talked about at the beginning of this chapter is an activity in which you ask Jesus to take you to a memory that caused you pain. I learned this strategy through *Transformation Ministries* as a part of their *Issue-Focused Ministry*. In Chapter 14, I will share more about this ministry as a resource. This specifically works for people with PTSD from some type of trauma because trauma victims tend to suppress memories that have caused them pain. Over time, it is as if those moments never happened. We forget the memories, or at least it seems we have forgotten them because we avoid thinking about them. But, the pain that they caused, whatever emotional damage they did within us, still very much exists. This is exactly where my anxiety stemmed from. We need Jesus to remind us of memories that caused us pain, so that we can hand over those memories to Him to heal in us. The thought of doing this was scary for me for obvious reasons. No one wants to revisit painful memories. But, Jesus won't heal what we don't hand over, and we can't hand over what we don't remember. Therefore, I had to go back thirty years and relive the time my mother died and the years that followed.

I revisited the little girl that struggled to understand life without her mother. I also had to relive my dad remarrying very soon after. I had to relive the confusion I felt, the physical pain that loss can cause, the anger, the sadness, the fear that everyone I loved would die soon. I also had to relive the loss of my mother's sister, an aunt on my dad's side, and my great grandfather, all within a couple of years of my mom dying. These deaths compounded my anxiety concerning losing people I loved. While reliving them wasn't easy, God is so good. He took me to those memories. I buckled over in tears. And then, the healing started to come.

After God takes you to revisit certain memories, you ask Him to show you where He was in those memories. This is a way of believing in Deuteronomy 31:6 that states, "I will never leave you or forsake you." You physically shut your eyes and ask God where He was. After all, He says He is always with us, so He is with us in the worst moments, as well as the good.

Visually, in every memory, He was there, right there feeling my pain, giving me strength. He was there in the pain where the devil was trying to do harm. God was there, so later, when we are ready to hand over that pain in exchange for healing, He knows exactly from what we need to be healed. His presence in my painful past was so comforting to me. I asked Him, "Lord will you take the pain of this memory? I'm so tired of carrying it around." And He did.

To better clarify this experience, because it's hard to put the presence of the Lord into words sometimes, I will give you an example of one of the memories He took me back to and how seeing His presence there was comforting.

The first memory God took me back to was the night my dad woke me up to tell me my mom had gone to heaven. It's important for me to tell you here what memory I had of this night before revisiting it with Jesus. The actual facts of that night are that my dad, in tears, was holding me, and he was whispering the best he could without falling apart that my mom had gone to heaven.

I also remember the exact thoughts that ran through my mind at that moment, "It's going to be okay. You have to be strong for your dad." You see, I knew what heaven was—I knew it was the goal for everyone. My mom had taught that to me. I knew she was with God and that wasn't anything to be sad about. The fact that my first thought was that I needed to be strong for my dad may sound sweet or heroic in a sense, but it stole any permission I might have given myself to grieve the way I needed to.

It was the devil stepping right in and putting a huge burden on me by giving me a mission that I would never be able to accomplish. It was a lie that I needed to be strong for my dad. That is what Jesus does for us. He is our strength. The devil had me believing I needed to take on Jesus's role. I carried that burden of responsibility throughout my entire life. It was the initial lie that changed me from being someone who shares their emotions and admits their struggles to someone who lives by the motto, "I'm always okay."

This is pure speculation, but I would bet with 98% assurance that the devil whispered that exact same lie into my dad's ear at that moment. If I am correct, that lie was the catalyst for why my dad and I would never really talk about my mom, dying or living, for over a decade after that night. That simple but powerful lie warped the way I would understand and react to sadness or pain, and all that happened in one moment when I was eight years old. That's the sneakiness and cowardice of the devil. He preys on helpless children and grieving families. That's why God needed me to revisit the memory of that night, and the vow I made to myself.

When I revisited this memory with God, I saw the exact scene as it was, with my dad holding me, but I saw Jesus with His arms wrapped around my dad and me. Seeing this as an adult allowed me to grieve that moment with Him. I just rambled on to Him how I actually felt that night, how I was scared, numb, how it felt like the breath was knocked out of me, how I wanted to be in heaven with her, how I had no idea how I was going to live the rest of my life without her. All of those feelings that I actually felt in the moment but didn't express because I was supposed to be strong for my dad just poured out of me. And because I now saw Jesus in the memory with me, I knew that He knew I felt all of those things back then. It made it very easy to ask Him to take all of that pain. Immediately, I felt the relief, the lifted weight, the freedom from the burden that I couldn't be weak and the suffocating feelings of sadness. It was like a hole in my heart was closed. It was beautiful.

After the relief of this experience, I wasn't afraid to use this strategy of revisiting memories for other painful moments anymore. I felt an urgency to revisit them and hand the pain over to Him. Piece by piece, I started to feel a little more whole, when before I had felt broken and empty. Healing from this process felt like a rebuilding of my heart. He restored what was broken by removing the pain.

Invite Jesus into your memories, into your pain. Let Him reveal moments where you have been hurt, and you don't even realize you are carrying around the pain from those moments. Be brave, have faith, trust Him. He was always there. He never left your side. He was there when that person hit you, when that person died, when that relationship ended, when that addiction caused you to do stuff you never would normally do, and on and on and on. He was always there. He never left you. Let Him heal your pain.

Reflection Questions:

1) How can the *Feelings Wheel* help you recognize and name the emotions that you are feeling at any moment?

2) How can handing recognized emotions over to God in prayer release you from continuing to feel a negative emotion?

Next Steps:

Try the *Feelings Wheel* activity for multiple weeks in a row to become familiar with the process. It will also help you become familiar with what emotions you are feeling and why. The more you recognize your emotional state, the more you will know what emotions you need to bring to God in prayer or talk about with a therapist, counselor, trusted friend, or mentor. Over time, you will become more comfortable expressing your emotions in the moment, in whatever way works best for you, and then you can begin to replace any negative emotions with how God feels about you or your situation.

Chapter 7—Forgiveness: The Game Changer

This chapter is about anger in disguise and its connection to unforgiveness. This is a tricky one for sure. And full disclosure here, this was and still is the hardest part of my healing process to reveal, understand, and hand over to God. Its roots lie deep and many are hidden, requiring true self-reflection, time, spiritual maturity, and prayer to be revealed.

For starters, I did not know that anger and unforgiveness were related. I thought that I could be angry and forgive at the same time. Here was my train of thought: I forgive such and such because I know that I have been forgiven by God for a million things I shouldn't have done. I am forgiven, therefore I forgive. He gave grace, therefore I give grace. However, once I thought I had forgiven someone, I would still have this anger toward them, and I couldn't seem to let go of that anger. I felt a need to carry the anger as a reminder that they were not to be trusted, and I had to be careful around them. If I let go of the anger, then I was letting my guard down, and setting myself up to be hurt again. My anger was ammunition, stored and ready to fire when needed. Unfortunately, that was my logic.

Eventually I learned I wasn't just angry, I was bitter, and that was what was keeping me from truly forgiving. There is a difference between bitterness and anger. Anger can show up in a moment and then leave. Anger gives warning signs that it is arriving like feeling hot or sweating, an increased pulse, and slowly losing your sense of calm. Anger causes a reaction that lashes out, rages, screams, or can even bring you to tears in the moment. Anger needs to be released. It is that knee-jerk reaction that can be triggered in an instant by being around a certain person, words someone says, thinking about a specific situation, plans not working out, or being treated unfairly. The list is endless.

Anger is apparent in young children, and it comes out as temper tantrums. When children become angry or frustrated with a situation, feeling, or person, their anger shows in the way they misbehave, get physical, or cry. As we grow up and mature, most of us learn strategies to control or subdue our anger in the moment, like walking away from a situation, avoiding certain people that constantly make us angry, and refusing to engage in unrestrained displays of anger. As adults, most of the time, but definitely not all of the time, we can control how we react when something makes us angry by recognizing the warning signs. However, as previously stated, anger needs to be released. So, although we may be able to control our anger in the moment, later it will rear its ugly head if unresolved.

Bitterness is the aftermath of unreleased or unresolved anger. Bitterness seeps into a person's soul and spirit, taints it, and begins to control our way of thinking and reacting to life. It can show up unexpectedly in the form of skepticism, sarcasm, judgements, unfounded fears, isolation, and mainly, an inability to trust. Anger is a healthy emotion given to us as a reaction to evil. Bitterness is more than an emotion—it becomes a filter by which we perceive the world. Bitterness puts a division between our spirit and soul by changing our thoughts, attitudes, and eventually our character.

If we don't feel angry in a particular moment, we tend to be unaware of the bitterness. This is important, so please hear me— no feeling or manifestation of anger has to exist in a moment for bitterness to exist. Hence, a person can be completely calm, easy going, and quiet, but eaten up with bitterness. Anger can be seen; bitterness can't always be seen. Bitterness, which is the product or leftovers of unreleased or unacknowledged anger, is what the devil uses to do his dirty work. The bitterness is the poison. Bitterness has a fantastic memory, holds onto everything, and feeds our grudges. Bitterness remembers those moments from our past, the last thirty years or so for me, and secretly uses them to change who we are. Bitterness is the devil.

I find this extremely important concerning children. When children are not allowed to release their anger through healthy discussions, drawings, journal writings, meditation, exercise, etc., then that child will carry the anger, and it will eat away at their innocence and joy, and it will begin to change them. Bitterness will take root in them. It will eventually be expressed in a way that may seem to outsiders as irrational, unfounded, and dangerous when compared to the situation in which it is expressed. I saw this with many students, in many situations, for many reasons when I was a public educator. Pure rage and hate would seem to come out of nowhere from students over very small, insignificant situations, but for whatever reason those situations triggered some type of bitterness that was stored in them. Think about some of the news stories concerning anger, hate, bullying, vandalism, killings, and suicides from children. There were signs along the way that these children were hurting and carrying bitterness toward situations that had happened or people that had taken advantage of them, but they weren't given or allowed a voice to express their anger in safe, mentored situations. Bitterness over time is very toxic in the way it changes people and their perspective on life.

Suppressed anger, which leads to bitterness, will keep us from being able to forgive. Here's how it works. Over time, when the bitterness toward a certain situation, political view, person, job, illness, or some other scenario has been in us long enough, we are changed to a new way of thinking, and forgiveness isn't a natural option. We don't recognize that we even need to forgive because we have now become comfortable with, used to, and fooled by our new way of thinking. We will even defend our new way of thinking. The thought that we need to forgive goes against the very person that we have become. To admit that we need to forgive means we must admit that we have suppressed anger that has led to bitterness. This takes extreme self-reflection to recognize and make the connection between unforgiveness and anger.

We can't forgive until we choose to change how we see and what we believe about a situation, person, feeling, etc. We have to flip the switch on the bitterness and reprogram our minds. We need God to help us do this. We have to start praying to God to help us see people the way He does, love them the way He does, and help them the way He does. Once God renews our mind, then we can see that we have not truly forgiven them or released them from the grip of bitterness, and we will want to do that for our own sake and character development. The bitterness will not go away and true forgiveness will not come without the transforming of our minds with God's help. But, it starts with recognizing when, where, how, and why the anger started, why it is unresolved, and how it turned to bitterness. Then, we must make a choice to forgive, in spite of all of that.

In therapy I was asked to write down some of the things I was angry about. I've shared a few of these in the following journal entry. Although I was asked to make a list of things I was angry about, it actually was a list of things I had become bitter about. There were feelings of resentment and unforgiveness underlying my list. The point of sharing this is to show how deeply rooted the bitterness had become, how long I had carried it, and how it truly affected my perspective. You'll notice the "What I'm Angry about List" is mostly from my childhood, ages 10 to 18, and not any recent events. This speaks to the bitterness that had taken root over thirty years.

* * * * * * *

Journal: What I'm angry about...

• *I wasn't allowed to have a voice or talk about my emotions.*
• *I wasn't raised in church after my mom died, so I wasn't shown the biblical way to handle dating, friendships, marriage, relationships, money, prayer, and peace.*
• *I'm angry that with my mom's death, I lost an entire side of my family because she wasn't there anymore to keep us close to her relatives.*
• *I'm angry that my dad lost the love of his life, and it broke his heart. It felt like I lost a little piece of him, too, the day we lost my mother.*
• *I'm angry that my dad got married so soon after my mom died. This marriage interrupted my grieving process for my mother, which I then carried into adulthood unhealed. For what it's worth, I think the exact same thing happened to my dad. We didn't heal because she was replaced too soon.*
• *I'm angry that the woman my dad married never talked about my mom or seemed to have any compassion that I lost her. It was like I was supposed to forget her, and that felt disrespectful to my mother. I was angry for both me and my mom.*

* * * * * * *

(Sidenote: The woman my dad married and I have now reconciled our relationship and discussed any anger that had, for me, turned to bitterness over the years. This is true for my dad and me as well. However, this is a book about my journey so transparency is necessary, which is why I included all of the above anger statements.)

I learned a lot from this activity. There is something authentic and raw about admitting that we are still bitter about things from our past. You will be surprised that what you thought was anger actually has turned into bitterness. If you feel vengeful, embarrassed, resentful, or blame people or events from your past for problems in your life now, you're bitter.

But dig deep. Let yourself feel the bitterness, and you will find that at its core is excruciating pain. The pain causing the bitterness is what God wants to take from you. Once I realized how hurt I was from all of the pain my "anger list" actually caused me, I suddenly was able to see past my bitterness and acknowledge my pain. I asked God if He would take that pain and heal me so that I truly could forgive, let go, and love again. He did. I did. Game changer!

Here are a few Scriptures that speak to this topic and show you the Bible calls for us to leave anger and bitterness behind:

For our struggle is not against flesh and blood, but against the rulers, against the authorities, against the powers of this dark world and against the spiritual forces of evil in the heavenly realms.

Ephesians 6:12 (NLT)

Get rid of all bitterness, rage, and anger, brawling and slander, along with every form of malice. Be kind and compassionate to one another, forgiving each other, just as Christ God forgave you.

Ephesians 4:31-32 (NLT)

See to it that no one falls short of the grace of God and that no bitter root grows up to cause trouble and to defile many.

Hebrews 12:15 (NLT)

Do not judge, and you will not be judged. Do not condemn, and you will not be condemned. Forgive, and you will be forgiven.

Luke 6:37 (NLT)

Jesus said, "Father, forgive them, for they know not what they do."

Luke 23:34 (NLT)

Reflection Questions:

1) Do you struggle with unforgiveness or a lingering anger toward someone that you thought you had forgiven?

2) Do you feel that you have become bitter by not releasing your anger to God?

Next Steps:

Make a list of things you are angry about from the past. Ask God to search your heart and reveal any unresolved anger that has changed your perspective about people and life. Come back to your list in a week or so and look at it with a new perspective. Are there people or events on your list that you need to hand over to God, forgive, and have Him change your thinking toward that person or event? Hand it over to God so He can begin healing you in those areas.

Part 3: The Battleground

For though we live in the world, we do not wage war as the world does. The weapons we fight with are not the weapons of the world. On the contrary, they have divine power to demolish strongholds. We demolish arguments and every pretension that sets itself up against the knowledge of God, and take captive every thought to make it obedient to Christ.

2 Corinthians 10:3-5 (NLT)

Chapter 8—Guilt, Shame, and the Secrets We Keep

The concept of shame, guilt, and keeping secrets became important to my healing journey because I started noticing that I wasn't always honest about things that I had done or that had happened to me. I also started to notice that other people were not being completely honest about their lives either because everyone seemed to only share the happy, positive moments and nothing negative or vulnerable. This train of thought, the idea that we are only supposed to share the parts of our lives that seem productive, successful, and functional, was a big reason I didn't want to go to therapy or receive healing from my past. I didn't think that it would be acceptable to share my struggles, the aftermath of my past, my insecurities, or the bad life choices I had made.

Also, I knew that therapy dealt with problems, but which problems? I didn't know which secrets I was supposed to expose and talk about and which ones were socially unacceptable to bring up or could affect the way people viewed me, my credibility, etc, even in therapy. Though therapy is between just you and the therapist, I knew once I exposed myself in therapy, I would no longer be able to avoid my issues the way I had in the past. Eventually, I would have to address a lot of these issues with family and friends.

I also didn't want to be judged about things for which I already felt guilty or shameful. Even if seeing a professional meant they had to abide by a confidentiality clause, I was uncomfortable sharing what I had avoided talking about for so long. I think many people don't go to therapy or receive help for their healing because of this same reason—we don't want to share our secrets. I really started to wonder if we were all just living a lie, a fantasy life, a Facebook and Instagram life, that masks the real issues we need to be sharing with each other. Here are a few examples you might relate to that show how I feared exposure in private with a therapist, as well as in public with peers, coworkers, friends, and family.

I had a fear of judgement. Don't air your dirty laundry. Don't share your business. Keep personal issues private. These are just a few of the directions I had heard growing up. The message was that we are not supposed to talk about our problems, struggles, or negative emotions, and we definitely were not to share addictions, mental health issues, or failures because people would judge us. There are two reasons I grew up thinking that others might judge me. One, they will judge me because they are doing life better than me, and I am weak if I am having these problems. Two, people who are obedient to God, or that are doing life the "right way," are not struggling the way that I am. So, it is better to just keep my secrets to myself, so that I will not be judged.

Another reason we don't share our secrets is because of the guilt attached to them. We feel guilty for how we reacted, what we did, what we said, or what we ignored, and we know we can't go back and change our past. So, it is better to just keep the secrets to ourselves. Examples of these types of secrets can be cheating, starting a rumor, lying, doing something inappropriate under the influence of a substance, a suicide attempt, wild days in college, feelings of responsibility for the abuse or neglect we suffered as a child, and the list goes on. We carry around guilt about events from our past. Over time, this guilt turns into shame.

Shame is the feeling or self-talk we carry through the years after the guilt of an event. We may quit thinking about the specific event that we felt guilty about, but now we have this new sense of self shaped by shame because of the event. We have lower self-esteem, we are embarrassed by our actions, or we think of ourselves in a terrible way for being part of an event. Shame brings on self-loathing, self-deprecation, and overall poor self-worth. We form a secret from our guilt and shame, refusing to talk about the event to keep anyone from knowing what happened and our part in it. However, though we may not talk about our guilt and shame out loud, we repeatedly speak negatively and harshly to ourselves. We may ask for forgiveness through prayer about something we did that we feel guilty about, but usually, we forget to address the shame. We believe that we deserve that feeling of shame and all that comes with it.

Here is part of a blog I wrote on secrets that was published one year before I started therapy. I was beginning to question the secrets that I carried and was interested in understanding the mental, emotional, and spiritual damage the secrets were doing to me.

* * * * * * *

Blog post: Secrets and How They Destroy Who We are Meant to be
September 21, 2018

I love to have deep conversations with people, ponder life with them and dream. I don't hide my curiosity, and I am not scared to talk about hard things. Life is hard. However, I'm learning that I tend to talk about hard things in a general way, like they exist but as somebody else's problems. I noticed that when having conversations with people about deeper issues such as depression, addictions, death, etc., we would talk about them without talking about ourselves. It would sound something like this, "When people are depressed . . . Addictions get people when they . . . If so-and-so died." Instead of it sounding like this, "I feel depressed when . . . I struggle with this addiction . . . I'm scared that so-and-so might die." I blame this inability to be vulnerable half on society and half on my own insecurity.

So, the society issue first. The way we talk about addictions, anxiety, depression, racism, suicide, or any other dark topic has seemed to change in my lifetime. The change for me, especially in the South, is that it used to be socially and spiritually unacceptable to talk about these things, and if you did share you were struggling, you were condemned and made to feel less than, weak, or far from God. This is when we create secrets to hide certain aspects of our lives. This causes us to go into overdrive to hide these dark aspects of our lives, when we turn to our vice (whatever it is . . . we all have our thing) and completely indulge ourselves, usually privately. We spend money we don't have on things we don't need. We drink until we are numb and hate ourselves for it when it wears off, we let unhealthy relationships consume and destroy us, or we binge eat, or cut ourselves, and ultimately get no relief because the secrets are still there.

And now, in the age of social media and technology, it seems that everyone shares. We overshare about everything. The people of the world have found their voice and want to be heard and heard loudly. Our secrets have now become our excuses for bad choices we make, or people we hurt, or responsibilities we avoid. It sounds like this, "The alcohol made me do it . . . My parents divorced and it messed me up . . . I was bullied when I was young . . . I grew up poor without any parents at all!" When we go this route, we become our secrets. I want to make it clear here that the above statements are true in the sense that alcohol does influence us to do things we wouldn't if we were sober; our parents' divorces do mess us up, being bullied does change who we are; and growing up poor or without parents has a huge impact on our future. It's not that what we are saying isn't true, it's that if we only use these aspects of our lives as excuses instead of seeing them as areas that need healing, then we are still keeping the secret to ourselves that we are in huge amounts of pain.

My own insecurities have led me to ignore my secrets, which produces a negative outcome as well. Insecurity made me fear exposure and kept me too embarrassed to reveal my flaws. Secrets are not necessarily flaws, they are more like scars and pain, but they make us feel less than, incompetent, or weak. We feel like a flawed version of ourselves. Therefore, the insecurities that we may feel as the result of our secrets make it appealing to keep them hidden. It is easier to ignore them. We can have a sense of pride or arrogance sounding like, "I'm fine. I don't have anything to hide!" We can also turn any attention to the problems of others to avoid discussing or confronting our own.

There are many of us who choose to ignore our secrets or live in denial that we have any issues. This leads to living up to only a portion of our potential. We remain angry, sad, and ultimately unfulfilled. Many of us are just trying to get through the day without exposing our secrets, while secretly looking forward to our vice that numbs the pain caused by our secrets.

But, it doesn't have to be this way. I know God, grace,

forgiveness, healing, freedom, and purpose exist. I've had glimpses of it throughout stages of my life when I was searching for answers the right and only way, with God. And it was liberating, fulfilling, peaceful, motivating, enjoyable, and a light to others in need. When I really started to ponder this and ask God how I could actually get to a place of freedom and stay there, He revealed I had to quit hiding the secrets from myself and others around me. Once I realized this, like I really let myself accept that I wasn't as transparent as I claimed to be, as I thought I was, I started to really pray about why I kept secrets and how I could change.

Here is my takeaway—what if we quit talking about the drugs, the food addictions, the over spending, the cutting, the alcohol, the bullying, or whatever is the issue, and we actually talk about the secrets driving those behaviors, the secrets and darkness that existed before we turned to the destructive stuff to cope? What if it is easier now to say, "I'm an addict, or depressed, or full of anxiety . . . I had a bad childhood!" than it is to say, "I don't know how to really be me, so I (fill in the blank) . . . I know I have all these gifts, stuff I like to do and know deep down I'm actually really good at, but I have the lowest self-esteem ever, and I'm scared to pursue my gifts and instead of sharing those gifts with the world, I'll cover them up with worldly things such as success, substance abuse, money, or defensive reactions."

The gifts I'm talking about are those that God gave you that make you different from anyone else, happy, and full of joy every time you use them because you know it's exactly what you were wired to do. Painting, singing, writing, dancing, being a mom, being outdoors, teaching, helping others, fishing, playing sports, and on and on. These are the gifts that get abandoned, our potential gets crushed and unused, because we are working so hard to cover up our secrets.

* * * * * * *

I specifically feel like there is a "keep it together" mentality that adults (with careers, marriages, children, and responsibilities) are supposed to have that children and younger adults are not expected to have. It's as if you reach a certain age and you are supposed to suddenly have it all together. Adults take on this mentality and teach their children this as well. We groom our children for an adulthood where no one has time for soul searching, emotional problem solving, or sharing in another person's struggles. It is accepted that we have things we as people are not going to deal with or share because that is our past. We are grown now and need to focus on the present, not worry about the past. I would go so far as to say that we even hide certain issues from our spouses and closest friends who may think they know everything about us.

The problem with all of this is that it's a lie. We don't reach a certain age where we automatically quit struggling from the guilt and shame of the past. The secrets don't go away. Every single moment of guilt and feeling of shame we experienced as a child, if not properly healed, exists in us today as adults. It is definitely one of the major reasons why we have such a high rate of anxiety, depression, suicide, narcissism, and identity crisis in adults. Our secrets will eat us alive, completely crush our potential due to fear, taint our relationships, distort our self-image, and sadly rob us of our childlike nature. Secrets attempt to destroy who God made us to be. This is exactly the devil's plan. In the next few chapters, I will expose some of the devil's lies that contributed to me hiding my secrets.

Reflection Questions:

1) Do you worry about other people's opinions of you? Is there someone in particular, or multiple people, that you are constantly worried about what they think of you?

2) Do you constantly want to impress people or feel the need to put on a mask, so everything seems okay? How have you tried to do that lately?

3) Do you hold back and only give the world a censored version of yourself? Can you think of one example?

4) Are you afraid to try new things, take risks, or pursue new opportunities? What are some things you haven't done or opportunities you have turned down out of fear? They can be very simple.

5) Do you have a negative view of yourself? What are some negative things you say about yourself, even if it's just in your mind?

Next Steps:

Chances are some of the things you listed in response to the questions above are keeping you from living the life that you want to live. If that's the case, then you may have some secrets that need to be revealed, some areas you've been hiding where you need to be honest with God, a close friend or family member, or even a counselor. There is probably shame and guilt attached to these areas of your life that keep you from reaching your highest potential, feeling a sense of peace, and pursuing your dreams. Becoming aware of these secrets, maybe even making a list of them like you have started in the reflection questions, is your first step toward replacing the guilt and shame you carry with God's truths. Now that you know what you are hiding, you can begin to work through it.

Chapter 9—Spiritual Warfare

You might be surprised at how difficult it is to change your way of thinking when you learn a new truth that contradicts what you, maybe even minutes before, have wholeheartedly believed. There are so many lies the world (TV, social media, corporate America, the government, certain social groups, some churches, and even scarier, our own self-talk) will tell us. We don't even realize how we soak up these lies into our thoughts and souls as we grow up, until they become a part of our identity and value system as if we have always believed them. But, there was a time when we were our truest selves, before we had soaked up all the lies. Think back to your childhood, when everything was purer. There were truths from God that were part of our identities, but they were later replaced with lies as we got older. Things such as value judgements on skin color, social cliques, popularity, politics, and gender roles are a few examples. At some point as kids, we didn't care about these things as far as using these details to make value judgments about people and situations. These details just existed alongside everything else as facts, like the grass is green. As young kids, girls believed they could do all the things that boys could do. Skin color mattered to us as much as eye color or hair color in determining a person's value, so not at all. As young kids, we weren't as self-conscious, we didn't know who was popular, and we didn't wake up every day thinking we had to compete with others to be noticed or important.

Nothing reminded me of this difference between our childhood selves and who we become as adults more than teaching kindergarten. If you want to be reminded of what an unbiased and untainted worldview looks like, go sit in a kindergarten classroom for one hour. You will generally see little humans learning from each other, laughing, showing healthy emotions, and not having a care in the world about what anyone else thinks. Though I only taught kindergarten for that one year before moving up to teach fifth grade, I taught many of those same kindergartners in fifth grade several years later. It was the coolest experience as a teacher. I was so surprised at how core aspects of their personalities were still the same. The hyper and silly class clown was still cracking jokes. The kind hearted mama bear of the group was still taking care of others. The curious, focused learner still loved to learn. They were each beautiful to watch as they grew into the personalities God gave them.

Like these kids, we too started out exhibiting all the innocence and unique traits that God intended for us, until something or someone hurt us and changed what we thought. Someone came along and made fun of a quality about us that used to be special. A situation made us feel unimportant or rejected. Then, the negative self-talk started, and we began to believe new things about ourselves like we were useless or unlikable. These moments are where we replaced God's truth about ourselves with lies from the devil. He stepped in ready to pound that lie into our brains until we believed it and it became part of our identity, shaped our world view, and informed all our value judgments about others.

Everyone will have hurtful experiences in life. However, there are extreme cases that occur, such as tragedy, abuse, neglect, or wrong teachings passed down through caretakers or churches, and these will be the source of the lies an individual will believe. But, most of us can think back to a time before the devil got his lies in us when certain hurts, doubts, criticisms, and anxieties that consume us now just did not matter! The devil is good at what he does, but his influence over us only lasts until we learn God's truth, meditate on His truth, and let what God says replace the lies we have come to believe about ourselves, others, and our life. When we are free of believing lies, the devil is exposed as the destroyer and liar that he is. We learn to fight back against the destructive lies he plants through our confidence in God's authority, power, and truth. This is the beginning of spiritual warfare.

Here's the kicker with spiritual warfare, though. The battle is already won. God's truth will outlive the devil's lies when the time comes for this world to end as we know it. The Book of Revelation describes the end times during which the devil is defeated. When Jesus died on the cross, he died for our sins, so for those who believe in Him and receive Him as their Lord and Savior, their slates are completely wiped clean. God no longer remembers any of our sins. Although we may believe the lies of the devil, we are only deceived and that does not make them true. God's truth is absolute, and the devil is just trying to trap us into living miserable lives without the freedom of God's truth. That's what I mean by the battle already being won . . . once we are saved, the Holy Spirit's presence gives us the ability and perspective to look inward and begin identifying and getting rid of lies we have picked up over our lives, lies that have moved our identity and value system out of line with what God intended for us. Remember the devil is called the "Father of Lies," so, of course he wants us to believe, especially on our worst days, that we are powerless, defeated, and without hope. He wants us to believe there is no freedom or healing from our anxieties, addictions, and pain. That's exactly what anxiety, depression, self-deprecation, and hopelessness tell us. But it's a lie.

It's important to know that lying and deceiving are the very essence of the devil's nature. He tells us all the same lies, but tweaks them slightly for our unique situations. However, once we recognize the lies that the devil is telling us, he has no choice but to flee when we fight back with the truth of the Word that God gives us in the Bible (remember how I talked about identifying lies and replacing them with Scripture in the last chapter?). James 4:7 states, *Submit yourselves, then, to God. Resist the devil, and he will flee from you. Come near to God and he will come near to you.* The devil has already been defeated by the work Jesus did on the cross, and he knows it; he just doesn't want us to know it and use it against him. That's why he lies. His one and only plan is to get us to believe his lies instead of God's word and ultimately let the lies poison our view of the world, other people, and ourselves. The devil has no Plan B. This plan is how *the thief comes only to steal and kill and destroy* as stated in John 10:10. Lies steal God's truth from us, kill our potential, and destroy the purposes that God made us for here on earth. Although lies can change everything, the truth, when we find it again, can change everything too.

Let me say here that we can't fight lies with lies, even though you will see people using this strategy throughout society. You can see this happening when conversations between two people or political parties go in circles, with both sides barely listening to the other and only focusing on their own point being right. Those are lies of pride and negative competition coming out that the devil has put in us. People who can't listen to one another or disagree peacefully believe that they can only resolve conflict by pitting themselves against someone else. That other person must be wrong. Seeing others as an enemy to be overcome is the only way for their point of view to be heard and for them to feel accepted or validated. You can also see it when prejudices come out over skin color, religious affiliation, or sex. That's the lie of judgement wreaking havoc between people. The devil has convinced someone to judge another person and exclude or mistreat them based on one of these traits, and that person feels little or no conviction from the Holy Spirit as to how wrong that is. They are believing a lie so strongly about another person that they are drowning out the gentle whisper of the Holy Spirit convicting them otherwise. In most tragic circumstances, the devil even convinces someone that they should take their own life because of the lies they have come to believe. Sometimes suicide notes left behind reveal lies that a person believed about themselves, such as they are not needed or wanted, they are a burden to others, or they have a hopeless life stretching in front of them. The devil's work is evil, and he tries to corrupt anything good.

For me, the lies I have believed have manifested through my anxiety. Anxiety distorts my viewpoint of myself and my potential, so most, if not all, situations are uncomfortable, even if I am with the people I love best or doing activities I enjoy. The main lie the devil sells behind anxiety, from my experience, is that isolation is best. Isolation means I am safe from being uncomfortable and can avoid anything bad happening to me. Anxiety also means living with confusion and tension. After all, I am with people I love and having experiences I should enjoy, but I just cannot be at peace or feel secure. The devil loves for me (and you!) to believe isolation is the answer and wants us constantly confused or stressed about why we cannot just enjoy our lives. We tend to give up seeking solutions when we are constantly confused and frustrated.

I don't know what lies you believe. Hopefully, you got started on discovering them in the last chapter with the list you made. You might not struggle with anxiety like me. There are a ton of lies related to all aspects of our lives that we can believe, lies about finances, social status, success, marriage, and our children. The list is endless. Whatever your lies are, you must fight them with the truth, but there is only one truth and that is God's truth. All the truth you have gotten from studying, research, life experiences, what your parents or friends have told you, what you've come up with on your own, will not fight the devil's lies if that truth doesn't align with the absolute truth of the Creator. God made us. He knows every quality that He specifically placed in each of us. He has all of the truths needed, ready to go, to fight all of your lies. The good news for us is He gave us all the truths written in the Bible, if we read it, and He also speaks to us at any time through prayer. Here are a few truths and lies that I wrote in my journals as they were revealed to me throughout my healing process:

Lies I spent most of my life believing	Truths I have learned to replace the lie
Beauty is connected to wealth, status, clothes, style, looks…	*Your beauty should not come from outward adornment, such as elaborate hairstyles and the wearing of gold jewelry or fine clothes. Rather, it should be that of your inner self, the unfading beauty of a gentle and quiet spirit, which is of great worth in God's sight.* **1 Peter 3:3-4 (NLT)**
Nothing will ever change. People do not change.	*Forget the former things and do not dwell on the past. See, I am doing a new thing!* **Isaiah 43:18-19**

Compete with everyone. Be one step ahead. In order to be the winner there must be a loser.	*Do nothing out of selfish ambition or vain conceit. Rather, in humility value others above yourselves, not looking to your own interest but each of you to the interests of the others.* **Phillippians 2:3 (NLT)**
Worry about everything or you will lose control and fail.	*Seek the Kingdom of God above all else, and live righteously, and he will give you everything you need. So don't worry about tomorrow, for tomorrow will bring its own worries. Today's trouble is enough for today.* **Matthew 6:33-34 (NLT)**
I must use my own understanding, I need to sit in long periods of thought and make very carefully planned and calculated decisions.	*Trust in the Lord with all your heart; do not depend on your own understanding. Seek His will in all you do and He will show you which path to take.* **Proverbs 3:5-6 (NLT)**
I can't be healed.	*And you know that God anointed Jesus of Nazareth with the Holy Spirit and with power. Then Jesus went around doing good and healing all who were oppressed by the devil, for God was with him.* **Acts 10:38 (NLT)**

We serve a good God who does not condemn us for our sins, but shows us a new way to live. The devil will use our sins against us in the form of shame and guilt. If you don't hear anything I have to say in this whole book, please hear this: shame, fear, and guilt are not from the Lord. God knows we mess up. He knows we are sinners. That's the whole point of Jesus dying on the cross, making the payment for our sins, and giving us the opportunity to reconcile with God. The biggest lies that the devil will tell are those that keep you away from God out of shame, fear, and guilt. God is NOT mad at you as a person, though we can upset and grieve Him with our actions, just as our own children do us from time to time. God loves you.

Because He loves us, God will ask us to make changes to align our lives and thinking according to His Word. Doing so means we are being obedient. Obedience on our part is what will free us from the sin that follows believing the devil's lies. God gives us His Word, and the Holy Spirit gives us the power we need to make the changes necessary to stop believing the lies of the devil. The Holy Spirit generously offers His power so that we can replace old, deceitful ways of thinking with God's truth and ultimately be free and healed. Please know that this is a process, a journey, and it will take time, effort, support, and resources. Later in this book, there are specific chapters directly addressing a list of different resources to support you. They are the same resources I used.

For me, it's taken many, many years to accept that I wasn't a constant disappointment to God, but rather the object of His affection whom He was trying to free from lies. The lies of shame, guilt, and fear cut real deep and in my opinion, are the biggest reasons we run from God, living life only half alive. These three prevent us from seeing God for who He really is, someone who wants to restore joy to our lives. Therefore, the lies destroy our hope. But, hope is still alive and found in God's truth. We also must share the truth with each other. Remember, the devil is already defeated. He just doesn't want us to know that.

Reflection Questions:

1) How have you changed from who you were as a child? If you don't remember how you were as a child, ask someone who might remember and who you trust to tell you positive things about yourself.

2) Are you ready for healing? If your answer is no, not yet, or you aren't sure, what do you think is holding you back? Is it worth it to stay where you are now?

3) Are you willing to take the time that it may take to reveal the lies that you have been believing and replace them with what God says about you and this world? If yes, what would you need to change in your life/schedule now to make time for this process?

Next Steps:

If you have made it this far in the book and you answered yes to questions two or three above, then you are ready to be healed. By now, you should have thought enough about how believing lies has changed you and have a better understanding of some of the issues, experiences, trauma, or lies that you personally need healing from. If you haven't journaled or written down anything concerning your own need for healing yet, this would be a good time. Once you have your list, go to God in prayer and ask Him to reveal your next steps toward healing.

In chapters 14 and 15, I have listed different resources that you might consider using as you take your next steps. You know how you learn best and what environments in which you are most comfortable learning and sharing. God will whisper to you when the time is right, if you continue to seek Him in prayer, and He will reveal which resources are right for you. Spend time seeking God in this area, and be expectant that He will answer. I have been praying for your healing.

Chapter 10—Exposing Generational Sin

This chapter includes the most valuable lesson I have learned so far in my healing journey. If you were to ask me the most important piece of advice I have to offer concerning anxiety, I would tell you to fact check your thoughts, beliefs, and value system against Scripture. Thus far in the book, I have shared a lot of my personal self-talk, doubts, and fears that concerned me. Now, I want to share how our unfounded, unbiblical, and distorted perspectives and beliefs about what matters in this world and our role in it are just as damaging as fear and self-doubt and cause their own anxiety. The anxiety stemming from unbiblical beliefs does not necessarily come from trauma or negative experiences but from lessons taught to us by people we love or worldly information that we choose to trust instead of the Bible. We give credibility to perspectives that are inconsistent with God's truth.

Many of us go through life never questioning the value system we carry, what we believe is important, or what is true. We do this for many reasons such as: we may find it disrespectful to our parents to challenge the truths they taught us, we may feel more comfortable believing what is the norm in our culture or group of friends, or we just are lazy and don't want to look too closely at something we might need to change. Consequently, we may even refuse to question our belief system when it is not working for us, is making us miserable, or is changing us into someone we don't even recognize or like. Most of the time, we stick to what we were taught by people we respected and trusted, such as parents, coaches, teachers, and churches, without ever going to Scripture to fact check our beliefs with God's Word. This is dangerous and irresponsible. This can damage the way we choose to live our lives. When these tainted and distorted versions of truth are passed down to our children they are called generational sins. This does not only apply to children we raise, but to those we mentor, coach, teach, or influence their thinking in any capacity.

We have a natural born tendency to question things and be curious about why things are the way they are. This is very apparent in children who question everything with big, excited eyes because they are trying to learn about the world they live in. However, many times, we as adults respond to them with, "Because I said so . . . That's just the way life is . . . You're too young to learn about that . . . We'll talk about it later . . . Don't question authority!" The message this teaches children is that everything is the way it is, and they just need to accept it without question. While there are times these answers are appropriate, they are often our default in situations we aren't sure how to handle or when questions are asked that we don't know how to answer. We use them as an escape hatch to avoid engaging with our children on certain subjects or working through complex issues with them as growing individuals.

We often fail to teach our kids how to problem solve on their own, go to the Bible for answers, or ask God through prayer for insight. I rarely, if ever, remember being asked as a child what I thought about something or how I would handle something differently. I do remember however, as a child, one specific response I got when questioning a Sunday school teacher about something in the Bible that I didn't understand. While I don't remember my question exactly, her response was, "We don't question God." There was no further explanation or attempt to explore my question. Immediately, my perspective of a loving, inviting Father God was changed, and I pictured Him as someone who lacked compassion, disliked teaching, and certainly did not invite any questions. This view could not be further from the Father God I know now or the one the Bible speaks of.

The more I read my Bible, the more I noticed that it was full of people questioning God and going to Him for understanding and wisdom. Any responses to children that do not invite them to engage with us concerning the truths they are building their lives on will leave them with the impression that they should never evaluate what they are being taught. Most of the things people teach us were taught to them, but they might never have checked their value system against Scripture and altered it if they found inconsistencies. It is often easier for us to continuously reteach what we have learned without stopping to do a real inventory of what we're passing on and how it lines up with God's Word. We don't consider the damage the lies are actually doing when we pass them on.

The worst part is, we are not trying to be malicious and actively harm the next generation or someone we're instructing. We just don't take the time to go before God and really look at what lies we are carrying around in order to replace them with His truth. The passivity on our part of evaluating our beliefs against Scripture is a trap laid by the devil. He wants us to keep passing down lies without question, never replacing them with God's truth. This makes his job easier because if he can convince one person to believe his lies, and they pass those lies down to their children, then they are now doing his dirty work for him. He can move on to the next family. After all, John 8:44 states, " . . . when the devil lies, he speaks his native language, for he is a liar and the father of lies." The devil is on a mission to fill our minds with lies and make sure they are spread far and wide.

However, it's not just what our family members or close mentors pass down that influences our belief system. Things like the availability of higher education, chances to travel or be exposed to different cultures, or opportunities to attend churches that share a different message than what we grew up hearing also play a role in shaping our values, either positively or negatively. The people who influence us, as well as how often we are exposed to diverse experiences, will impact our belief system. I tend to think if we always experience what we've always known, we are not as open minded and relatable because we never have our preconceived notions and misconceptions challenged. Our narrow mindedness shows up in our belief system about people, ideas, and places.

A few common areas in which we often harbor ungodly lies are in our beliefs about spirituality, the economy, our government, and social interactions with others. These are all areas that impact our day-to-day lives, and when we express our ideas about things like race, identity or image-related issues, spending money, "correct" political choices, what should be taught in public education, or how a church should be run . . . we are giving a good window into what informs our belief system. And I've come to recognize that some of our values might not be biblical.

Ultimately, no matter what the influential people in our lives teach us or what our experiences, or lack of experiences, make us think, our biggest responsibility is aligning our belief system with Scripture. We will all have moments or people that push us outside our normal comfort zone and bombard our minds with information and opinions we could make part of our belief system. They can be positive like when travel, education, and even new friends who help us develop more complex perspectives on life. They can also be negative if we are exposed to ideas that just don't line up with the Word of God. However, thanks to Scripture, we can put all our beliefs through an easy "truth test" and adjust when we are in the wrong, so there's no confusion about what God intends for our lives.

The question is . . . will you? There comes a moment in many people's lives, if they dare to reflect on what they believe to be true, that they find many of the things that they have spent their whole lives believing were actually never true to begin with, according to the Bible.

Furthermore, some realize they have spent a major part of their life focused on and influenced by ideas and values that never felt important or true to them. It's as if these values have guided their whole lives, but deep down, they never truly felt comfortable taking ownership of them. For example, if a child is taught that a certain race is superior to another, he/she may grow up accepting this belief, but maybe in his/her soul, they feel that this can not be true. Specific to my life, I chose for many years to buy into the idea that self-sufficiency, independence, and control of my life was the only way to live. This mentality made me feel isolated, unable to rely on others or ask for help. I constantly strived to uphold the "Fake it 'til I make it!"mantra. This is not a biblical concept. The Bible teaches dependence on God and others, fellowship with believers, and an "iron sharpens iron," (Ecclesiastes 4:9-12) or "two are better than one," (Proverbs 27:17) approach. God repeatedly emphasizes humbleness, not arrogantly insisting you need nothing from Him or anyone else.

So, why is it important to fact check our beliefs against Scripture? Why was this lesson so important to me and my healing journey? In essence, what we believe is our own individual truth. If you are a Christian, whether a new believer or a seasoned one, and you believe the Bible to be true, then your individual truths must align with the Word of God. Anything that does not is an ungodly lie. There are no gray areas. Jesus is the Light and the Truth and came to set us free from any ungodly lies. God addresses every single topic He finds necessary for us to understand about life on earth, our purpose, and our life after this one in the Bible. The Bible is our roadmap for what is true and never changing. Scripture is not any different today than it was before or than it will be in the future. We can use Scripture to examine our thoughts, values, fears, desires, pleasures, questions, and concerns to find out what lies we believe. That is one of the reasons God gave us the Bible and encourages us not just to read it, but to study it.

Now that I'm a mother, I find it extremely crucial to fact check my thoughts and ways with Scripture. If what I believe is a lie passed down to me through the generations, and I choose to pass it down to my children, then I have entered the realm of generational sin. This is exactly where the devil wants me and everyone else to be, stuck in a cycle of passing down lies. He is the deceiver and the father of lies. Our mind is where he does his dirtiest work in disguise. I found it critical throughout my healing process to "Take my thoughts captive and submit them to the Lord" through prayer and aligning them with Scripture as instructed in 2 Corinthians 10:5. This has changed everything for me concerning my self-talk, self-image, life goals, political views, and standards for raising my children.

The miraculous phenomenon of being a human is that we are rational beings, as much as we are feeling beings. God gave us the ability to think critically and make decisions concerning our lives. What we believe will directly affect how we choose to live our lives, what we spend our time doing, and what we value. We owe it to ourselves to make sure our belief system lines up with the Word of God because He knows what's best for us. He is our Creator. He will not force us to live by His Word but offers it for our protection from the lies of the devil. If we just assume everything we believe is correct, then we may very well be living our lives based on lies and reap the consequences both daily and in eternity. These lies will exhaust us, condemn us, confuse us, depress us, and ultimately have us live a substantially less fulfilling life than God intended us to live.

Reflection Questions

1) Are there lessons you have been taught that deep down you have questioned their validity?

2) Are there beliefs that you hold that you are not sure line up with the Word of God?

Next Steps:

I suggest taking the time to evaluate your belief and value system. Think about what is important to you concerning family, work, what you do with your free time, your goals, what you teach your kids, and how you view yourself. I am not talking about what you hope for the future or how you wish things were but how these things are really playing out in your life right now. Now, pick a few of these things and start comparing them to God's Word to see if you have any areas that aren't lining up with Scripture. It is likely that you have started to believe a lie and need to start replacing that lie with the truth.

Part 4: Life After Healing

You intended to harm me, but God intended it for good to accomplish what is now being done, the saving of many lives.

Genesis 50:18 (NLT)

Chapter 11—Understanding Surrender, Calling, and Purpose

I spent years in church and reading Scripture, but I could not understand these three words: surrender, calling, and purpose. I did, however, seem to have an innate understanding and willingness to walk in faith. I will explain the meaning of each word in this chapter, comparing the way I understood them prior to my healing and how I understand them now. I will explain how the freedom that comes from being healed of anxiety and all the lies associated with it has changed and grown my understanding of these terms.

Surrender

At first, I was confused with what it meant to surrender my life to God. My former understanding of surrender involved a distorted view of control. I thought the act of surrender meant to give control over to God, and He would make whatever area of struggle I surrendered to Him go away. I thought I could do this through prayer and it would sound something like this, "Lord, I know smoking, or saying mean things, or fear is not from You. I know they are things that You do not want me to do, so I surrender them to Your control because I know I can't control them on my own." Then, I waited for them to be "poof" gone. I expected for the urge, the temptation, the desire, the circumstances or environments in which they showed up to no longer have any appeal to or influence on me. When this didn't work, I assumed I hadn't really surrendered, I was a weak Christian, or I wasn't doing something right. I later learned this expectation just isn't biblical; therefore, my assumption of finding an instant cure was another one of the devil's lies. That is not to say God doesn't do those sorts of miraculous interventions, but we often see in the Bible people walking out a process of healing through growth and change, not always an instant freedom from their struggles or circumstances.

Now, I understand surrender very differently. As I continue to walk out my healing journey, get closer to God, and trust Him, I've learned the tremendous love behind the word surrender. As I previously understood it, surrender had God working like Santa, a genie in a bottle, or a wishing well to grant my desire at my command. However, there are major faults with that way of understanding God's character and our surrender. Under my old model, God was serving me instead of me serving Him, and I stayed in control, while having the illusion that I was handing it over to God. My "poof" method did not require a relationship with God, just a quick prayer, desire, or wish list that I would bring to Him to grant. That version of surrender did not require extensive patience, trust, or faith in God's character. The assumption was that I would control the conversation with God about my needs, and He would answer by handling what I needed, taking what I didn't want, or providing me a life instantly free of temptation, struggle, chaos, pain, or loss.

As I said, every bit of that mentality conflicts with the Bible. Over and over, the Bible reminds us the devil will tempt us to do wrong, pain will come, and loss is inevitable until the day we die. Chaos is the aftermath of a broken and fallen world since Satan tempted Adam and Eve in the Garden of Eden, and temptation, pain, and loss all lead to struggle. That is exactly why we must surrender to God daily, giving Him all the chaos, pain, fear, temptations, and challenges in our lives. Daily, we must trust God to strengthen us in the midst of the chaos, not in the absence of it. We need God to heal our hearts when the pain comes, and teach us the lies that the devil brings to us, so we can recognize them and replace them with His truth. Lasting dependency on Him, not momentary encounters, is exactly what God wants from us. He wants a daily, developing relationship with us. In return, He will protect us in this life, strengthen us in our pain, help us see the calm and good in the chaos, and change our understanding of our addictions, hang-ups, and disorders, so we can overcome them with His help and in His timing.

I now see that surrender is a continuous act. It never ceases until our time is done here, and we reach heaven. That is His promise. Heaven is our hope, our gift, our inheritance, and the place the devil can't touch us. However, we each have a reason for being here. There is a reason why we are experiencing our unique life as it unfolds. God is a creator with purpose and intention. He is organized and eternal, and we were created for an eternal purpose. Once I became healed from my past, my present and future could, for the first time, become something not to fear, but to get excited about. I wanted to step into my calling.

Faith

Once I began to understand surrender, I wanted to surrender each day, despite my battles, and start hearing God. I wanted to know what He calls all Christians to do and specifically what He was and still is calling me to do. The first thing I learned is that calling requires faith. This was a relief to me because faith is a word I have always understood. I think it is one of my spiritual gifts. I have the ability to believe in what is not seen in circumstances where some find it hard to see even a glimmer of hope. I think that faith developed in me at a young age, after the passing of my mother, because I chose hope, God's word, and the reality of heaven instead of a negative, doom-filled outlook on life. I've never doubted the existence of heaven or God, even when I didn't understand much about them. There was always just an assurance in me that heaven and God were real, and God was good. I have always been very comfortable throughout the years acting out in faith. I seemed to always believe subconsciously, if I prayed about it and went for it, God would show up. Faith is actually what kept me wanting to understand surrender, calling, and purpose. My faith was always on fire. I would keep trying new things, acting out in faith, praying in faith, believing that God would help me understand how to surrender and lead me to my calling and purpose.

I need to clarify how I have the gift of faith while also suffering from extreme anxiety. This may seem contradictory or confusing because if you have faith, how can you have anxiety, right? Before my mother passed and I was seven years old, I asked Jesus to come into my heart and be my Savior. I was saved and baptised, and these decisions were not from any pressure put on me. I knew what I was doing, and I made the biggest, most genuine decision of my life. I remember the whole process like it was yesterday.

My mother died the year after I became a Christian. Talk about divine intervention! This is important because it wasn't long after my mother passed that I quit going to church altogether. No one in my immediate family was going to church, and I guess as a young child I quit seeing the importance of going if the adults in my life were not going, so I quit asking anyone to take me. I would learn later, as a young adult, that church is very important. The years that I didn't go to church, I started getting further away from God. There ended up being about a ten-year span before I started diving into the Word again and about a twenty-year span before I started attending a church again. However, the gift of faith was always with me.

Even though the gift of faith was mine, I didn't always know I had it because no one had ever taught me what a spiritual gift was. So, when I was a young adult, I would use the word intuition instead of faith. I would always say I was really in touch with my intuition, the small, still voice that guided me when I was frequently doing things that seemed confusing or risky to others. For example, I abruptly changed from a fashion design degree to a philosophy degree, moved once to a new town alone on a whim, ended toxic relationships without ever looking back, and applied for positions for which I didn't seem qualified. All of these decisions, based purely on what I used to call intuition, worked out. Even now, I am writing a book with no idea if anyone is going to read it, but I am doing it on faith based on what God told me to do.

Something has always been driving me, giving me this boost of confidence or assurance that the decision I was making was the right thing to do, even though following through on the decision could simultaneously spark high anxiety. So, anxiety and faith have existed in me, side by side, my whole life. It was as if the devil and God were both fighting for me to do their will or believe what they each wanted me to believe.

The way I see it now, the gift of faith was God's way of saving me every day by giving me hope and reassurance that He was still with me, despite the anxiety. It's like God gave me the gift of faith, so I would continue to pursue Him or try new things, even though the anxiety was terrible. I did believe all the things the devil was telling me about myself at one point, but part of me believed even more strongly that God would show up if I just kept seeking Him in faith.

To be honest with you, looking back now, if God hadn't given me the gift of faith, I don't know that I would have continued to pursue or believe in God after my mom passed because I wasn't around other believers to encourage me to believe and seek Him. However, because of the gift of faith, I always sought Him. I always had this innate drive within me to keep seeking Him, to understand Him, to find my way to heaven. My mother gets complete credit for teaching me in the eight years she was with me as much as my little brain could hold about Jesus our Savior. Her teachings contributed immensely to my choice to accept Him, and in return, he bolstered my faith during my period of wandering away.

Below is a portion of a blog I wrote explaining my understanding of faith.

* * * * * * *

Blog post: Faith?
April 2019

The answer is on the other side of the question mark, but inside the question mark is where the magic happens!! So, jump into the question mark. Dive deep. Swim around. Wrestle, cry, get angry, dream, be expectant, and then step out to the other side of it.

What Scripture says:

Now faith is confidence in what we hope for and assurance about what we do not see...By faith we understand the universe was formed at God's command, so that what is seen was not made out of what was visible.

Hebrews 11: 1-3 (NLT)

The Lord himself goes before you and will be with you; he will never leave you nor forsake you. Do not be afraid; do not be discouraged.

Deuteronomy 31:8 (NLT)

...strengthened in the faith as you were taught, and overflowing with thankfulness.

Colossians 2: 7 (NLT)

"According to your faith let it be done to you"

Matthew 9:29 (NLT)

The Question Mark

What I have learned about faith is that God will meet you inside the question mark. The question mark symbolizes the crossroads in our lives where God is prompting us to make a change, start over, give something up, or do something radical that doesn't seem rational. These promptings from God to "make a move" in an area of my life always begins, for me, with a whole lot of questions, doubts, and confusion. This is what I'm calling "being in the question mark."

Where We Find New Perspectives And Grow

Inside the question mark is where a lot of work on our part is done but with His guidance, prompting, and teachable moments. Inside the question mark is where we change and become the next best version of ourselves. Clarity will not necessarily be found here . . . only questions, lessons, curiosity, and some (or a lot) of frustration. This is where we choose to learn or continue our old ways, grow or stay the same, change or refuse to change, accept that His thoughts and ways are bigger and better than ours or keep controlling, become humble through vulnerability or guarded and protective of our old selves.

At the end of the process, after we have spent the time we needed questioning God, He will have a question for us . . . "Do you trust Me? Will you take the next step?" If the answer is yes, we will step forward out of the question mark to the next stage of our lives already designed by God. This is where faith becomes a verb, an action, not a noun.

The Unknown

God's will for your life is in the unknown. This is the hardest part for me. I like spending time with God learning and praying. I DO NOT like giving up control and walking into unknown, unfamiliar territory. It is scary and unpredictable for me, however, it is very predictable for God because there is no unknown territory for Him. The lack of purpose in our lives is because we refuse to step out into the unknown in faith.

* * * * * * *

Calling and Purpose

From my experience through this healing journey, God reveals what He has called us to do when we are healed. The more we act in faith, the closer we get to discerning and becoming comfortable with our calling. It is a part of maturing spiritually. Once God shows you that what you need healing from is what He wants you to use to heal others, life starts to have meaning and purpose.

However, for the longest time, calling and purpose were distant phenomenons to me. For many years, I believed that a calling was only for "really good" Christians or the people who go into ministry. To a certain extent, the way I understood calling was correct in that the people who were aware of their calling were close to God and had spiritual maturity from walking out their faith with Him consistently. God does call the chosen to serve Him in the ministry of the Church as a whole.

I didn't realize that any who believed they were saved by Jesus Christ were chosen and called, which meant I was a candidate for having a calling and a purpose. The devil has the ability, if we don't recognize his schemes, to distort the truth just enough to confuse us. Just this small misunderstanding of calling, being chosen, and doing ministry was the difference between knowing my life had a God-given calling to give it purpose, and living the best I could until I died and went to heaven. Under my old self, I would have just "tried life the best you can until you die" approach. Under my new mindset, I see myself as someone with a calling and purpose.

God's calling on your life has existed from day one; God always knew what He was calling you to do on this earth to serve His purposes and reveal His glory. For many of us, He wants to heal us first, replace the lies of the devil with His truths, and then He will reveal how He has called us to use that healing. I wouldn't have even had the vocabulary, insight, or knowledge to express to anyone a couple of years ago that God would call me to write a book about anxiety after a year of healing me from it. I didn't even know how to attach the word anxiety to my life until recently, hence, that the extent of my fear and worry was anxiety. But, God knew. God always knew that this was His plan for my life—that if I would take a huge leap of faith, trusting and believing that He would heal me, He would then reveal how this was always His plan to begin with.

Once we know what we are called to do here on earth, our life starts to have purpose. For example, once I surrendered my anxiety to God for His healing, He prompted me to start writing this book. I didn't quite see the purpose in it when I first started, but I knew God was calling me to do it. Not until I really began to recognize that the anxiety was gone and I no longer believed past lies, did I realize I had a new life free of my past. Only then did I see how God was turning harm into good. Only then did I see that because He healed me, I actually had a story to share in the hope that my testimony could show others that healing was possible if they pursued it. As Paul referenced in 2 Corinthians 16-18, a veil had been removed from my eyes, and I was free to see clearly. Under my old way of thinking, there was only pain, but after healing, I see my life as having a purpose.

I challenge you to surrender with faith, pursue healing, receive your calling, and serve His purpose for your life. What a beautiful process!

Reflection Questions:

1) Do you know what God has called you to do in this life? If not, have you asked God if there is an area in your life that He wants to heal that may be acting as a "road block" between you and understanding your calling?

2) Maybe this is not God's timing for revealing His calling on your life. If this is the case, have you asked God to align your will with His so that when the time is right, you will be prepared to carry out whatever His will intends?

Next Steps:

Answering the above questions should open up a great conversation between you and God. Take time to talk to Him about Faith, Calling, and Purpose. Ask him your questions and take time to listen to His answers. God may answer your questions through His people by additional resources. Talk with others that you know have a relationship with God and ask their thoughts on these topics. Find books or lectures on these topics. The more you understand God's Word on these topics, the easier it will be to bring your questions, desires, and needs to God in prayer.

Chapter 12—Whatever it Takes

There is a statement that many of us claim as a major part of our value or belief system, which is: nothing, absolutely nothing, is more important than your relationship with God and His purpose for your life. Often, we find this statement easy to say, and we say it with firm confidence. The implications of this statement are what we tend to overlook, disregard, or even choose not to believe - if nothing is more important than our relationship with God then that means not even our spouses, children, parents, extended family, jobs, social lives, or past mistakes. None of these things matter more than God and His calling on our lives. Even if you think you believe this to be true, more than likely your everyday schedule will tell you something different. I know mine did when I first looked at it. Many of us spend more time on every other part of our lives than on seeking God, serving His people, and taking the time to be in His presence, so He can reveal His purposes for our lives. I don't have any hard numbers on the statement I'm about to make, but I assume it is very common just from looking back over my own life that many people who claim they are Christian don't find time to do any of the following on a regular basis: go to church, read their Bible, pray, or find ways to serve others in Jesus's name. I've been one of these people. The years I did not give God my time were the years that my anxiety was at its worst. My life felt meaningless and chaotic, and I made a lot of choices I wish I could take back.

We were made exactly how we are for a reason, all our desires, life circumstances, hopes, dreams, talents, quirks, experiences, and pains were given to us or allowed to happen to us for a specific reason, an eternal purpose. If you live your life without knowing the purpose God intends for it, you will be filled with unfounded, relentless, consuming, debilitating worry. Below, I have listed all that God has taught me about figuring out and stepping into His calling on my life. I have found that believing the statements below, arranging my life so that it shows that I believe them, and choosing to act out their truths in faith has dramatically strengthened and directed my walk with God into what He has called me to do. I believe that if you will apply them to your life, as you see fit, then your life will start to reveal your calling and purpose as well.

This life is a test. Heaven is real. It is eternal. It is our forever home. This life is short in comparison to eternity and is a test that prepares us for eternity. The concept of tests exists in our lives from day one. Babies and young children have milestones they are supposed to accomplish as they grow and mature, such as eating solids, crawling, walking, talking, learning to share, manners, writing, reading, and other things. If you are a parent, you know how excited you get when your child accomplishes one of these goals, but you also know how each goal takes practice, failures, guidance, and some struggle. School-aged kids are required to learn large amounts of academic material, some of which may be outside their interests. They are in school when they also might rather be doing something else. Tears while doing homework, kids excited to miss school for holidays or breaks, and academic struggles show that learning can be discouraging, uncomfortable, and even painful at times. Competing for sports teams or social groups, the nerves that come with job interviews, hardships of marriage, struggles with parenting, financial responsibilities, coping with sickness or loss, all of these challenges show that life is full of tests.

Some we pass, some we fail, some we choose, some we never would have chosen, some feel worth the pain, and some we may never understand why they happened on this side of heaven. Regardless of whether we chose the challenge, obstacle, or tests that are in our lives or if they were placed there by the devil with hopes of destroying our will and distracting us from what God has planned for us, God will use all of these types of tests to grow our character for His planned purpose in our life if we let Him. We must acknowledge this truth for it not to be merely wasted time, struggle, or pain.

You were made for an eternal purpose. Once you accept that life is a test in order to build character through patience, endurance, and persistence, only then will eternity make sense.

The tests in our lives are preparation for our eternal life. The whole point of being here for this limited amount of time on earth is to prepare us for what comes next. Think of it as training. We accept this concept in life all the time when we say things like, "Did you practice or study for the test . . . I'm training for (work, a marathon, the military, etc.) . . . Preparation is key . . . nine months of pregnancy allows the baby to grow and the parents to prepare . . . practice makes perfect . . . If you fail, try it again!" We accept that we have obstacles to overcome in this life to achieve our goals or get something we want.

It is important to see our life here on earth as preparation for eternity in Heaven. God gives each of us certain skills, gifts, and callings for two reasons: to spiritually groom, enhance, pursue, grow, and train us to be more like Jesus and to share our gifts and callings with His children that are lost and don't know Him. With our gifts and callings, we bring them closer to Him. Both are for His eternal purpose in Heaven.

Get yourself right. If there is anything that is holding you back from getting close to God and learning your purpose here on earth, take time to heal in that area, unravel any insecurities or lies that might be holding you back, soul search, and self-reflect to get a grasp on what is keeping you from being exactly who God made you to be. It could be addictions, anxieties, obsessions, doubts, fears, insecurities, or something else. Use some of the strategies in this book or from other books, groups, websites, retreats, churches, therapists, friends, or family members and start to research and understand any hang-ups you may have. Make it a priority. Break the chains of your past, shame, guilt, or trauma, and walk in a new freedom that lets you seek your calling. This will be a process but start the process today. God is there waiting to walk through it with you. He is not mad at you, and He has wiped your slate clean through Jesus's death on the cross, if you choose to believe that, so you can come to Him for healing and guidance. He loves you, desires to spend time with you, and wants to heal whatever you hand over to Him. He will meet you exactly where you are in your journey and hold your hand as the healing process takes place.

Cut out all that doesn't matter in your life because focus is the key. I want to say that I by no means have this completely figured out yet, and I am still in the process of doing it myself. Removing what doesn't matter from your schedule will take discernment from God. God will reveal what in your schedule is taking your focus off of what He wants to do with your life. It has been a mental shift for me, and I am having to reprogram my understanding of what is a priority in order to consistently focus on what God wants for my life. Staying focused on what matters will require your ongoing dependency on God and having conversations with Him throughout the different stages of your life. The devil will seek to derail you, and if he can't make you disobedient or outright bad, he might try to make you busy. He wants you to avoid what God has for your life at all costs. I am just now starting to understand the importance of a focused, prioritized life without extra activities, people, things, and goals that don't align with my calling.

Our schedules and bank accounts reveal what is important to us. Where and what we spend our time and money on is where we place value and importance. Give these areas of your life an examination. If God is not a part of your life, then replace some of the areas of your schedule with Him. If God is not a part of your marriage or your time with your kids, then add Him in. If your money and time do not reflect any value for serving others, evaluate how you use your money. Reorganize your life with God as the center of all you do, focus on the things that matter to God, and cut out anything that is keeping you from hearing from God.

Again, I am still in the process of doing this myself. It takes time, and in fact, it's best to do regular evaluations of your time and money to make sure something hasn't slipped in. The process is not a one and done deal. What God tells you is fine today might be something He asks you to readjust later at a different stage of life. We should always be checking in with God, so He can help us balance our life with the things He wants us to invest in and not get bogged down by those He doesn't. Don't get fooled into thinking that what God asks you to get rid of will be all bad either! Sometimes we are busy or distracted by "good" things but not "God" things. In fact, "good" things can be harder to get rid of than obvious sins. Spend time with God and other believers regularly, so you can get His help and wise counsel while you go through this process.

Spend time with God every day and seek Him in prayer. This is the part of our healing journey and spiritual maturity that is our role in which to take action. Matthew 7: 7-8 states, *"Ask and it will be given to you; seek and you will find; knock and the door will be opened to you. For everyone who asks receives; the one who seeks finds; and the one who knocks, the door will be opened."* God will not force you to seek Him for healing because we have free will. He'll gently nudge you through the years, but ultimately, He wants us to acknowledge that we need Him. We must ask Him first.

This is the only way to stay on track. Every day, we must spend time with God. Every day, we must talk to Him in prayer. If you keep a constant dialogue going with God, you will become more comfortable and accustomed to seeking Him before making decisions, and eventually, you will start to hear the Holy Spirit regularly speaking guidance and purpose into your life. God will not heal what we don't bring to Him. You can't bring stuff to Him for healing that you don't recognize exists in you and needs to be healed. God will reveal these areas to you if you seek Him and spend time with Him.

Keep going even if it's painful. As I've already mentioned throughout this book, the healing journey will bring up raw emotions, insecurities, fears, doubts, and past memories that you will not want to experience. No one likes to experience any of those negative emotions, but experiencing the buried pain is part of the healing process. There is no way around it. You must make a commitment to yourself that you will continue seeking healing through the rawness that will be revealed along the way. This is not a foreign principle in our society. Athletes, medical students, and military personnel all get broken down to their weakest state just to struggle and then be built back up to a stronger state. Revealing all of your secrets and pain will feel like a break down, and in a sense, it is. Stay with it. God taught me most of the lessons He wanted me to learn when I felt like I couldn't handle any more. Hang in there.

Whatever it takes! Own your healing and pursue it like your life depends on it because it does—at least the life God intends for you anyway! Cry out to God over and over with your questions, fears, and pain. He will take it, and over time, He will replace what the devil meant for harm in your life with good. Seek healing until you know you have received it. Expect God to be the Healer, Provider, Comforter, Redeemer, and Savior that He says He is. He wants us to put full faith in the promises He made to us in His Word.

Reflection Questions:

1) How can you readjust your schedule or your priorities to make room for your own healing journey with God?

2) What can you add into your schedule to enhance your healing journey with God?

Next Steps:

Ask the Holy Spirit to reveal any areas of your life that may need to be put on pause or deleted completely as you commit yourself to "whatever it takes" for healing.

Chapter 13—Healed

How do you know when you are healed? I feel this is a question that I would want answered if I was reading this book. I can see it in how I think, how I feel and pray, and how my perspective on life has changed. In order to be genuine and realistic, though, I want to divide my answer into two different categories: what healing looks like on a daily basis for me and what it does not look like. My hope is that by honestly sharing how my life is different, as well as ways it is not, after healing, you will be encouraged and filled with hope to truly pursue God for healing in whatever area of life has kept you from feeling free, passionate, brave, and able to love.

I am now more aware of my thoughts. I recognize when an anxious thought, fear, or lie is being developed in my mind, and instead of letting it wreak havoc on my sense of peace, I take the thought captive. I don't take my thoughts lightly any more, and I don't treat them as absolute truths just because I thought them. I now question, ponder, and challenge every thought with Scripture, prayer, or by talking them through with other trusted Christians. If the thought does not align with God's word, then it just doesn't have value to me any longer. I toss it out. I don't believe it. And I won't pass it on to my children or repeat it as truth for other adults to pass along.

This does not mean I never have anxious thoughts! It does not mean I always know exactly what is a lie and what is the truth. However, I now have the strategies, insight, and knowledge of what to do with thoughts stemming from fear or worry, and I use these tools to keep my thoughts in check. I go to therapy a lot less than I did throughout my intense healing journey, but I still go. I go about once a month now or whenever I feel I am struggling with an issue. With my therapists, I work through any thoughts that I am having trouble determining if they align with the Word of God or if they are the devil trying to slip in a destructive lie. My thoughts now are filtered—they no longer have free range to pop in and out of my mind, unquestioned, as truths.

I am now free to feel, and I am not scared of my feelings. Before I was healed, my own feelings made me anxious. It was like I knew there were so many undealt with feelings buried in there that one tiny emotional feeling would have a snowball effect and unleash all of them. I felt no control over my emotions, and I hated this feeling. For example, just watching a movie about a car wreck or someone losing their mother would have me in hysterics. So, I hardened my heart over time. I refused to feel. I used to think this was a superpower in a way- that I had this ability to not feel emotions when others did. I was wrong. Through the years, I had given up the freedom to feel because I was scared to feel, but now things are different. I invite my feelings to come as they are, when they want, in whatever form they want, and around whomever they choose to let loose. Someone who suffers from anxiety like I did doesn't have the freedom to feel like others, but now, I have this freedom with my healing. Furthermore, I *choose* to acknowledge my feelings as they come instead of stifling them, and then they move on. I am no longer carrying the baggage of unresolved emotions. I take my feelings to therapy and talk it out, I share my feelings with my husband in a way I couldn't before, and I bring my feelings to God for healing and ask Him how He wants me to use any of the emotions I feel. That is freedom.

What it does not mean is that I'm happy all the time or I don't experience negative emotions. I am no longer scared of my own feelings, even the negative ones. This is huge for someone with anxiety because fear and worry feed anxiety. But, if I am no longer scared to feel, then the devil does not have that control over me to give me intense anxiety. Now, I know how big my God really is. As a paraphrase from Pastor Chris at Church of the Highlands, "I take my big problems to my bigger God, and my problems no longer seem as big!" I'll even add that when my problems seem smaller, the devil seems even smaller than the problems themselves. My prayer life has completely changed in this process, too. I turn to God to heal my emotions in the moment or keep bringing whatever emotion I am struggling with to Him over and over again until I get a resolution. Even if the resolution is that it's not time for a resolution, and I need to be patient with what He is teaching me in the process. Usually, it's because He sees a way bigger picture than my human mind can grasp. But, if His response to me is no resolution now—then, I accept that and move on.

My total perspective on life has changed. I don't think from an anxious mind any longer. I don't look at life as scary, something I have to control, or something I need to isolate myself from. I now know God truly heals in the way He promises in Scripture. I'm excited about life again. I want to share my story. I want to be honest, raw, and forthcoming with the "real me." I truly believe there is nothing that I can't face in this life with God, and believing anything else is just a lie from the pits of Hell. In a way I couldn't before because of my own pain, I now notice when people aren't being honest or are struggling with anxiety. My level of empathy and compassion has skyrocketed for those who feel trapped by their inability to take off their mask, to let go of their facade for fear of failing or being judged. That is why I am writing this book. I pray with everything in me that my story breathes hope and life back into someone who desperately wants to feel free and be exactly who God made them to be.

My changed perspective does not mean I think I can do this on my own from here on out now that I am healed! This is huge. Please hear me when I say that the second I think I don't need God is the second the anxiety will come back. Thinking I don't need God is the open door that will let the devil back in with a vengeance. But, this is not something to fear. This is knowledge, the meaning of "the truth will set you free," as referenced in John 8:32. I know I walk side by side with God, a God that is my Father, Friend, Counselor, Healer, and Provider. That is my new perspective. He knows I'm going to mess up. He knows I have a stubborn nature. He knows me because He made me. I will need discipline, I will need to be reminded of this healing year, and I will need accountability partners surrounding me. Continuing my forward momentum is not a journey that I intend on facing alone. I have a lot of great friends, mentors, and family surrounding me that I know will help me as well. I hope you will start your own healing journey and bring others along with you as well. We all need people to share in our struggles and to remind us we are not alone.

Healing is absent from any arrogance and requires me to humbly submit myself to God. Healing invites divine intervention from a loving God who wants nothing more than to fill our hearts with His truth. I will forever be grateful for His healing.

Reflection Questions:

1) In this chapter I talked about what healing looks like for me now on a daily basis. How would your life be different if you had strategies to recognize your anxiety when it rears its ugly head?

2) Which part of my healing shared in this chapter appeals to you the most and why?

Next Steps:

Use your answers to the above questions as motivation to start or continue your healing journey. Your vision for your own life without anxiety is what should be your focus. We all have lives with different responsibilities with different priorities and anxiety robs us of accomplishing those with peace and confidence. This is a good time to really try and visualize what your life would look like if you had strategies to manage your anxiety and took the time to bring it to God for healing. Use this vision of a life of freedom to feel, participate, and prosper in the life God intended for you.

Part 5: We Will Not Heal Alone
Resources to Help in Healing

Then Jesus said, "Come to me, all of you who are weary and carry heavy burdens, and I will give you rest. Take my yoke upon you. Let me teach you, because I am humble and gentle at heart, and you will find rest for your souls. For my yoke is easy to bear, and the burden I give you is light."

Matthew 11:28-30

Chapter 14—Finding Your People

Initially, the hardest and scariest part of the healing journey for me was reaching out for help. I genuinely believed in the beginning of my healing journey that I was a broken and flawed person and was alone in my battle with anxiety. I was filled with guilt and shame and embarrassed to share my struggles. I am a teacher, writer, churchgoer, wife, and mom. I feared that sharing my story through my blog, therapy, and church small groups was going to affect my credibility as a professional, and a mother, and would harm my reputation in general. I know now all of that was the devil's way of guilting and shaming me into living a lie and refusing to seek help. However, I did not know this truth for most of my life, and that is exactly why I never sought outside help. It wasn't until I was desperate that I sought help, regardless of the consequences, because I was determined to get healed and be the mom my son deserved.

In this chapter, I share with you my different sources of outside help and support. I also include information for you to check out the different books, ministries, and other resources for yourself. However, I must tell you I was successful in using these other resources because I went to God first to guide my healing. He helped me get on the right track and was intimately a part of all my other experiences. All of these resources I point out served their own purposes in my healing, and I highly recommend them all. Still, none will be as effective as God Himself if you include Him in the process.

God

God is the Healer—everything else, whether a book, a ministry, or a counselor, is just a resource He provides to assist in our healing. My conversations, cries, questions, and fears about wanting, needing, begging for complete healing started with God. I needed Him onboard every step of the way, or I knew any outside help I sought or efforts I made on my own would only provide temporary relief and not actual healing. I knew this because I had already tried to battle my anxiety on my own through: denial, antidepressants, wine, packed schedules, sleeping pills, yoga, church, prayer, Scripture, and more. All of those things worked just enough to carry me temporarily from one season of life to another, but my anxiety always lurked just below the surface, waiting to creep back up. My anxiety never actually went away; I just ignored or heavily managed it at different periods.

The level of healing I needed required complete surrender to God, full disclosure to Him about my pain, anger, regrets, worries, and fears. Once I got to that vulnerable place with Him, He gently started to put the resources (that I discuss below) in front of me. He knew I would need all of them to help me relive a time of my life I barely remembered, my mother's death and the events that followed. The time of my life where a huge piece of my life was stolen - my mother's presence and guidance - and I was left with anxiety. This is the one resource that must come first. You must meet with God the Healer before you seek help anywhere else.

Therapy/Counseling

Professional Christian psychiatrists, psychologists, and church counselors are trained to help people unravel their issues, to listen and guide them toward healing, and to provide their recommendations for the patients' next steps. I have always believed that their knowledge is helpful, but I never felt comfortable enough to seek their help. Furthermore, the few I did see when I was younger either stared at me and waited for me to speak, put me on medicine, or focused on issues that didn't seem important or helpful to me. My perception that therapy was unhelpful as an adult was based on these experiences when I was younger. As a child, I did not have the vocabulary or insight to share my deepest and darkest feelings, and I never felt comfortable doing so with the particular people I saw. While some school counselors tried to help me, and I really enjoyed talking to some, they didn't have the time allotted in a school day to get me to a place where I really opened up about the emotions with which I struggled. All of these unsuccessful experiences, along with the cliché in our culture that only damaged and emotionally weak people see therapists, kept me from considering therapy as an option as an adult, even when loved ones suggested it would help.

My perspective toward therapy eventually changed. I matured enough to realize I needed help understanding my anxiety. Also, I realized there are many, many therapists and counselors available and I had the right to "shop around" until I found one that met my needs and made me feel comfortable. Lastly, I was desperate to heal, and I no longer cared about any stereotypes around therapy or had any hang-ups about sharing my secrets. Frankly, at the point I sought therapy, I didn't give a damn what anyone thought about how I went about healing; I just wanted and needed to heal. Some of the loved ones in my life supported me when I said I was going to therapy, and some shamed me or told me to not tell anyone. Neither side played a role in my decision to stick with therapy. I went for myself, and I didn't need anyone's approval.

I consider my therapist and my counselor as friends now. They lovingly walked me through some of my most painful memories, feelings, insecurities, and fears. I went to both of them for an hour a week for months until I had healed enough to go less frequently and was ready to move on to other resources they suggested to support my healing. I will continue to seek their advice any time I feel there are issues with which I need help. I consider both of them blessings sent from God and a huge reason why I am healed today.

Trustworthy, Honest, and Reliable Family and Friends

Not everyone that you love is going to show support, take time to understand, or empathize with your need for healing. Some will try to make you feel weak, ridiculous, or shameful for even needing the healing. I experienced this and it was hurtful. It will be most hurtful when you try and share this process with, reconcile with, or forgive those who took part in the trauma that you need help with, but pursue healing anyway. That pain, anger, and rejection you experience on the way is part of the healing. Don't hide your healing process - own it. Stand strong on the promises that Scripture provides that remind you that Jesus's truth, understanding, and acceptance are all that matters and are all the "go ahead" you need to seek healing, however long it takes and through whatever resources He provides. The loved ones that don't support you in the beginning or doubt your complete healing from God will witness it through seeing the changes in you. Don't go out of your way to force them to see the changes in you. God doesn't want us boasting or acting prideful or tossing out "I told you so!" to doubters, but He does want us to shine as a light into the world reminding others that God is still very much in the business of healing, miracles, and making us new.

For the loved ones who are supportive, that will pray for you or answer the phone when you are struggling through the healing (because this isn't an easy process), the ones that will cheer you on and remind you that you deserve to be completely healed, they are some of the most beautiful blessings throughout this process. They are needed. You will cherish their insight on what they have noticed about you throughout the years that you didn't notice about yourself. Many loved ones will be the rock you need when you are tempted to quit seeking healing because reliving trauma or sharing your secrets aloud gets so painful that you start doubting your ability to survive it. I pray blessings from heaven pour down on the family and friends that loved me and on those of yours that will love you through some of the darkest healing days.

Ministries

Shake the Sheep Ministries

Contact Information:

Shake the Sheep Ministries, Inc.
508 Heywood Street
Auburn, AL 36832
334-332-3325

Website: https://www.shakethesheepministries.com

How it helped me:

My counselor introduced Shake the Sheep Ministries to me as a resource to receive Issue-Focused Ministry (IFM). An IFM is something I had never heard of before it was suggested to me by my counselor. Basically, in a very condensed version, IFM is for someone who is dealing with a major issue in their life from which they want healing and freedom. For me, it was my anxiety. It is a three-hour prayer session, involving direct and intense spiritual warfare, that focuses on the specific issue a person chooses. Please look at their website as they have great, detailed information there.

It's hard to explain exactly what it did for me, but I will do my best because my deliverance was huge. Being vulnerable and engaging in spiritual warfare with God's power healed my anxiety. The day I left that meeting at Shake the Sheep Ministries, the anxiety as I had known it never showed up again. Hints of it would start to show up, but I had all of the tools to recognize it and hand it over to God immediately. My IFM experience was about three months into my healing journey. I was not healed 100% that day from all my root issues that laid deep beneath the surface of my crippling anxiety, but these root issues masquerading as general anxiety were now exposed. My anxiety was no longer manifesting in a way that was regularly disrupting my life, and I came out of this experience able to identify and focus on the deeper issues that needed healing.

While the anxiety is initially why I sought help and healing in the first place, the accompanying fear, shame, guilt, and doubt, was just what the devil had been using all of my years to control me. Anxiety was only the tip of the iceberg of what needed to be healed in me. Like I said, once the anxiety was removed, revealing the real root issues and trauma, God began to address and heal these in the months that followed my IFM session.

The big "aha" moment for me when learning about Shake the Sheep Ministries is that there were actual Christian-based ministries created for the purpose of helping people heal from past traumas, PTSD, and anxiety. For the first time in my life, I felt the comfort of knowing that there were other people out there struggling, seeking help, and finding healing. I was not alone.

Restoring the Foundations Ministries

Contact Information:

Restoring the Foundations Ministries
PO Box 1418
Mount Juliet, TN 37121-1418 USA
1-828-696-9075
Email: healing@restoringthefoundations.org

Website: https://www.restoringthefoundations.org

How it helped me:

After my IFM session, Restoring the Foundations (RTF) sent me audio messages for thirty days that continued to reinforce principles learned through the IFM. RTF recommended that I listen to one a day for the next thirty days. The purpose of listening to these RTF messages directly following the prayer ministry was to keep the focus on what had been healed, released, and surrendered in the IFM session. I was so grateful for these messages because they were short, to the point, filled with Scripture, and a continuous reminder of what I had overcome in the IFM session. The devil's lies don't become our personal truths overnight, and it's hard to replace lies with new truths on our own because the lies feel like the truth when we have believed them for so long. I really needed these RTF messages to remind me of what were my old ways of thinking, alongside the lies the devil had fed me, and now what were my new biblical, godly ways of thinking. Basically, the RTF messages kept me filled with Jesus's truth for thirty days until I believed what Jesus said instead of what the devil said.

Transformation Ministries

Contact Information:

Transformation Ministries
100 Missionary Ridge Drive
Birmingham, AL 35242
205-991-4988

Website: http://trministries.org

How it helped me:

Shake the Sheep Ministry and my counselor recommended the TM School of Ministry for me to attend. The school offers four courses taught over four semesters on topics such as inner healing, spiritual warfare, and breaking strongholds. I was curious about the classes, and being the learner and teacher that I am, a classroom setting was an environment in which I was comfortable.

I now know there are three main reasons God wanted me to take these classes:

1) The trauma I experienced happened over thirty years ago, and I needed to learn which issues added to my anxiety. I needed help exposing the devil's lies attached to that trauma and replacing the lies with biblical truths. I did not have the knowledge I needed about anxiety, trauma, and PTSD for healing.

2) I needed to be around others who were experiencing similar anxieties, who wanted to be healed, and who were seeking truth about how certain life experiences had changed who God made them to be. I needed to be reminded throughout my healing process that I wasn't alone. I needed accountability partners who knew my secrets and would check on me each week to make sure that the devil wasn't trying to guilt or shame me into giving up on my healing.

3) I needed God to see that I was serious about seeking Him and His people for healing. I was willing to step out in faith even if I was embarrassed or scared. God needed me to learn from His other children, to let them love me, and to get comfortable taking off the mask by bringing my issues to light in front of others.

Small Groups

Small groups, in many churches, have replaced what we traditionally call Sunday School. These groups are put together by church members centered around personal interests such as sports, prayer, book studies, cooking, marriages, parenting, crafts, finances, and other topics. There are other groups that focus on mental health issues such as anxiety, trauma, death of loved ones, depression, eating disorders, PTSD, etc. These are regular people, just like you and me, that want to be educated, healed, and supported. Most of the people who attend are first timers. The groups align their discussions or curriculum with the Bible but bring people together through a shared interest, activity, or topic.

Small groups are a great way to ease yourself into fellowship with other believers who have experienced similar life events as you. You may go a couple of times and stop if you do not feel the group is the right fit, you may go just to listen and not share at first if that makes you more comfortable, or you may feel inclined to share your story in hopes of helping someone else. In some groups I have been very vocal and in some I have just enjoyed learning from the other people. You will usually find someone in the group (particularly one of the group leaders) that you have never met, but relate to and feel that they understand the issues with which you are struggling. Those will be the people who are willing to pray for you specifically throughout the group or answer a text on a day or night that you are struggling. Some friendships will last just for that group, and others will become lifelong relationships. It can be the beginning of surrounding yourself with Christians that want healing and support just like you.

Below, I share one of the small groups, Freedom group, that will educate you on some of the strongholds or lies that the devil has slipped into your thinking over the years. This small group's curriculum will give you the Scripture you need to replace the lies with truth in your life. Below, you will find information on Freedom group and other small groups offered by the church at which I am a member, Church of the Highlands. However, there are many churches that offer an array of small groups that you might prefer. You may have to look at what's offered by the church you attend or other churches in your community if there is not a Freedom group near you. Don't be afraid to ask a friend if they know of any small groups because their church could host a group you might find beneficial. What is most important is getting involved in a group with people and leadership that can support you.

Group Name: Freedom

Contact Information:

Church of the Highlands (Main Campus)
4700 Highlands Way
Birmingham, AL 35210
205-980-5577
info@churchofthehighlands.com

Use the website below to find out when these groups are offered, which location and time works best for you, and who to contact for that specific group.

**Church of the Highlands Website for Small Groups:
https://www.churchofthehighlands.com/groups**

How it helped me:

I have attended a Freedom group twice. Once in my twenties when I was single, and again about ten years later with my husband. The first time all of the material was brand new to me. I had never really heard of spiritual warfare, and I wasn't aware that a lot of the emotions I felt were lies from the devil. My eyes were opened over the course of the group to say the least, but it was a lot of information all at once. Also, I wasn't mature enough or self-aware enough to apply all of it to my life, but it stirred my spirit for sure, and I did find freedom in many areas of my life.

The second time I attended Freedom I had just had my son and was about two years out from surrendering my life to God for complete healing. This time I realized how far I had come in my walk with Christ from the first time I attended Freedom group. I was much more knowledgeable about the devil's tactics and the truth available to me in Scripture to combat the devil. Yet, I still wasn't ready to apply all that I learned to my life. I was still in denial about my anxiety and embarrassed to talk about my issues to the extent that I needed for full healing. Nevertheless, part of me was soaking it all up, laying the foundation for my future healing.

Both times I attended Freedom group, God was doing work in me by exposing me to the schemes of the devil. From my experience, I can assure you Freedom is a small group you can attend a few times throughout the years and learn something new each time. It is a great group to join to help you start taking inventory of some of the baggage, pain, shame, and guilt that may be holding you back from living the life God intended you to live.

My journey of healing is not over. It is just beginning because I have a desire to pay it forward. Although I am healed, I know many are not and God has called me to use my story to continue the healing journey with others, and I couldn't be more humbled and honored to walk out this calling with anyone who needs me. We are supposed to learn from each other, support each other, lift each other up, and love each other without judgement. I can't help but imagine a world where we all take off our masks, share our issues, make the decision to step into our own freedom, and then help others do the same. That is 100% my intention for this book. I've been praying so hard for you, friend. God's there waiting. You are not alone.

Reflection Questions:

1) Do any of the above resources appeal to your particular situation and why?

2) How could any of the above resources help you on your healing journey?

3) If the resources listed don't appeal to you, what type of resources do you think would work for you and why?

Next Steps:

This is a good time in your healing journey to begin researching or reaching out to resources that can assist you in healing. I would not have been able to unravel my pain, memories, or anxieties without outside help. Open this up in prayer and seek the Holy Spirit's discernment and wisdom concerning which resources are right for you.

Chapter 15—The Books That Changed Everything For Me

I want to share more resources that have helped me. I have read each book mentioned in this chapter to further educate myself on what would help me work through the layers of anxiety that unfolded throughout my healing. These are not novels - some are devotionals which require a little reading each day - others are topic-based that provided further insight into the issues discussed throughout this book. All were crucial to my healing.

Title: *The Bible*
Author: God
Topic: Everything that matters

How it helped me:
Let God speak to you. The Bible is the number one most important thing that exists on this earth. It is alive. It will speak directly to your situation, circumstances, feelings, struggle, or sin. The same verse will have multiple meanings throughout your life. You will never read it enough because it will always speak different meanings to you. It is the road map to life. I am confused, frustrated, and lost when I don't continue to read it. This world will not tell me what God wants to tell me through His word - on many occasions it will tell me the complete opposite. God's word is the ONLY truth. The world screams what it has to say (commercials, the news, social media, political debates, friends, co-workers . . . everyone has something to say and loudly), but God whispers His truths because He is a kind and gentle spirit, and for me a lot of the time, He whispers His wisdom to me through the words of the Bible. If I don't find some quiet time, shut out the world, turn all devices off, and draw near to His whisper by reading His word, I would miss some of the best secrets He wants to share with me just the way He knows I need to hear them.

Title: *The Circle Maker*
Author: Mark Batterson
Topic: Prayer

How it helped me:
This book revolutionized the way I understood and went about prayer. Batterson talks about praying big prayers in the book. He speaks about how if we believe in a big God then why do we pray such small, mundane, and submissive prayers as if we don't serve a miracle maker, dream dispenser, and purpose-driven God. Batterson suggests that our God is to us as big as our prayers are to Him. This book allowed me to step out of my routine prayer life and really come to God with everything on my mind and everything I wanted for the future. It gave me the freedom to ask so that I can receive as long as it was according to His will. This book was the beginning of me realizing that God never intended us to pray shallow, surface-level prayers, but to ask Him for miracles, the supernatural, and divine intervention.

Title: *Draw the Circle-The 40 Day Challenge*
Author: Mark Batterson
Topic: Focused Prayer

How it helped me:
This book is a forty day devotional that suggests we focus our prayers and pray them repeatedly for forty days . . . or "as long as it takes." It is the idea that God enjoys and honors prayers that aren't fleeting, but persistent. I actually have done this devotional twice. The first time was while I was single and becoming more serious about getting married and meeting the right guy. I realized that I hadn't actually taken this desire to God regularly and chose for this to be the forty day focused prayer that I brought to God. My first date with the man who would become my husband was about two months after I finished the forty day prayer challenge. The second time I did the challenge was when I started to write this book. I was praying for discernment about what to put in the book, God's wisdom, and mostly just reassurance that God wanted

me to write this book at all. So, needless to say, this devotional has guided me through two monumental decisions/opportunities in my life. Batterson is great at getting you excited about your talks with God, praying big prayers, and being consistent in prayer.

Title: *The Cure*
Authors: John Lynch, Bruce McNicol, and Bill Thrall
Topic: The world's way vs. God's way, Religion vs. Relationship, Fake vs. Real

How it helped me:
This book was a huge eye opener for me. It cleared up any misconceptions I had about how God sees me, my sins, my prayers, and my relationships with others. The book does a wonderful job of distinguishing between the "fake" version of Christianity versus what the Bible says being a Christian is supposed to look like. This gave me a huge relief because one of my "anxieties" was exposing my struggles with "church people." For the longest time I felt the shame and guilt of my past experiences, choices, addictions, and coping mechanisms, along with the fears that anxiety brings to most situations - I believed I was a "bad" Christian that just needed to have more self-control, will power, and strength. This book flipped the script on that idea and used scripture as its basis to state that concept simply is not true and that train of thought simply pushes us further away from God, which is Satan's purpose for placing those lies in us to begin with. The Cure gave me permission to be vulnerable with God, which is what He wanted and what I needed.

Title: *A Purpose Driven Life*
Author: Rick Warren
Topic: Purpose and Calling

How it helped me:
I read this book once in my early twenties and again just recently. It has sold around thirty million copies in over eighty languages. Those statistics should pique your interest. Warren does a phenomenal job laying out a forty day explanation of why we were created, how to align our life with God's purpose for our life, why a purpose driven life is the only life with any meaning, and the heavenly vision for our lives here on earth. After healing, I wanted to live a more purposeful life, tapping into God's calling on my life. I have this new freedom from being healed and released from the anxiety that has held me back for so long, and I want to live more intentionally, according to my purpose, and alongside other believers who want to do the same. This book realigned my focus and gave me the guidance I needed to tap into God's purpose for my life.

Reflection Questions:

1) Which of the books mentioned might help you in your walk with God or your healing? How could the books you chose help you?

Next Steps:

Start or continue your healing with God by using the guidance of other books. Books are my favorite way to break down any road blocks I may have in my prayer life, my understanding of what I may be struggling with, or my lack of hearing God. We are intended to learn from other Christians. If you don't enjoy reading, get the audio version and listen to it while you are in your car, taking a bath, working out, or cleaning the house. Make your spiritual well-being a priority by finding at least thirty minutes a day to heal and align yourself with God's truths. Other people's stories, conversations, and testimonies are a fantastic way to get the Word in other than just reading the Bible or going to church. Podcasts, conferences, YouTube videos, etc. are also great ways to hear other Christians' stories and lessons learned.

Acknowledgements

It takes a village, and looking back I see how God provided me with a village of people along the way to love me, teach me, and provide support through the years until I came to a place ready for healing. I would like to thank and acknowledge these people before I get to the people directly associated with this book. Here is a list of the beautiful souls God strategically and divinely placed in my life throughout the years.

My dad stepped up to the challenge that was handed to him of being a single parent. He is the only person on this planet who shares the intimate memories of our family of three before mama passed. A bond was created out of that brokenness between us. I love him more than life.

My cousins have always been supportive and my first best friends: Jill Darnel, Jeannie Peden, Jeremy Goslin, Brad Goslin

My cousin who is like a brother—Christopher Goree has been and continues to be by my side through the good, the bad, and the ugly. We have kept each other from feeling alone in some of the hardest stages of our lives, and there is no one who makes me laugh till I cry like him.

My Aunt Pam and Uncle Jimmy have always treated me as their own and loved me unconditionally.

Ashley Cahn and Jan Busby are not just my best friends but have been more like my sisters for the past twenty years. They know all my secrets and I know theirs. We love, encourage, laugh, cry, argue, and support each other in a way that has been fundamental to my stability throughout the years. God knew I needed both of them.

The Molpus Family has treated me as their third daughter and gave me a sense of family when I needed it so desperately.
Lisa Littlejohnn was my mentor and friend during my time in Birmingham.

Hall-Kent Elementary gave me a loving work environment to master the craft of teaching and grow as a young adult.

* * * * * *

God also placed some very special people in my life that directly led to my healing. Thank you to the people below for loving me enough to support me through a very emotional and vulnerable time of therapy and healing. I was so emotionally fragile during this time that I know I would not be healed if it wasn't for your love.

My husband was so patient through this process because I couldn't help but bring it home.

My church counselor (now friend) prayed for me and gently guided me through the unraveling of my past.

My kind-hearted, spirit-filled therapist gave me hope, strategies, and wisdom to carry home with me as I continued working on my healing.

Sayler Hammer, my editor, spent many hours chatting with me about how to turn my journals and story into something that others could use for healing as well.

Jim Buford gave me a deeper and more objective reflection of the book by showing me perspectives and angles of my story that I had not seen on my own. He turned my manuscript into a book by introducing me to Tina Tatum.

Tina Tatum, another editor, guided me through the publishing process. I was completely clueless as to how that worked, and I will forever be grateful for her wisdom and guidance.

And for anyone else who took the time to listen to me cry, get frustrated, and be confused over and over again before the healing started to settle in, I thank you.

In loving memory of David and Abbey Darnell.

About the Author

Shellie Goree Smith was born in Opelika, Alabama and grew up in nearby Auburn. She earned an undergraduate degree in Philosophy from Auburn University, an Early Childhood Education Masters and an Administration of Education Masters from the University of Alabama at Birmingham.

Smith worked as a public educator for eleven years and is currently a writing coach at a community college. She and her husband Jeff live in Auburn, Alabama. They have one son, Grayson who is two years old, and are expecting another son, Grant, in April 2020. The Smiths attend the non-denominational Church of the Highlands.